grace trail®

Find Your Footing and Move Toward The Life You Were Meant to Live

by Anne Barry Jolles

5 Steps Toward Your Best Life

What is Grace Trail?

Grace Trail is a simple process that guides you to find hope and possibility in the challenges and confusion of life.

You walk it for the sake of living your best and most courageous life.

Table of Contents

Dedication

This book is dedicated to my husband Jon
who has been my partner on this trail and
that has made all the difference in the world.

Preface
How I Grew Up

I think I was born old.

Grace has been waiting for me outside my door since I was a child. Growing up as the fifth child in a family of six in a small Irish Catholic family—where my mother was an alcoholic and my father didn't make it home much during the daylight hours—left a lot of space for some creative chaos to go on in our home.

Things were good for us when I was younger—before I turned 10 years old. I was raised like a duckling with six of us in a row. There was always someone in front of me to follow and someone behind, following me. We lived in a great neighborhood just south of Boston and, when things turned bad, there was always a back door for me to slip into. I could be in others' homes quietly and be invisible in their families. Many of my friends had at least one alcoholic parent but at least it wasn't *my* alcoholic parent.

I wasn't fully aware of the problems in our home until I was 12. Before that things just seemed normal—how everyone lived. It wasn't until I was in college and went to other friends' homes that I noticed that their parents did not always have a drink in their hand.

At one point, there were five young people between the ages of 12 and 20 in our home. We had three car accidents on one day. Anything that could happen, was happening. We all did some stupid teenage things, but I am not here to tell anyone

1

else's stories. But I did think I was in the crazy house. As bad and crazy as it all seemed to get, I tried to be the good kid, which is another kind of problem. I always had a job, friends, a boyfriend, volunteered, was a good student, and, of course, a cheerleader. I did everything I could think of to keep out of that house and not come home. I was usually met at the door with a report of just how bad it was in there today: "She's really bad ... you may not want to come in." So I didn't. I put all my energies into overachieving, trying to fix things, and trying to get the hell out of there—from which I am still re-covering.

I often tried to save my mother, whom I really loved. I re-member being 12 years old, making coffee and trying to force her to drink it so she would be sober when my father came home. Well, you know that never worked. I still can't celebrate Saint Patrick's Day because there has to be something bet-ter from my ancestors than green beer. This disease has left a huge path of destruction in its wake throughout my entire extended family.

I guess my father felt unreachable to me because I never tried to save him. Today I realize he was doing the best he could do. He withdrew from us and I didn't get to know him, al-though he was a great provider. We lived in a beautiful neigh-borhood with a beach and wooded area nearby. I am grateful that it was a safe place to grow up where we could be outside for most of the day. I thought my dad was always working hard but eventually realized he just stayed away to avoid it all. When he came home, he would hide from my mother. I couldn't blame him for that.

I can remember, with one of my older sisters, calling the hos-pital where they help alcoholics and asking if they would take her if we brought her. She was so drunk, so scary, and so mean that day. They said, "Yes, bring her in." They didn't make it clear that they meant to evaluate her. We told my mother that we were taking her for a hot fudge sundae and she jumped in the car. When we drove past the ice cream shop, she got the message but she was in the backseat of a two-door car and couldn't get out. It was a long ride there but nothing compared to the ride home. By the time we reached the hospital she was so full of rage that she had sobered up. She went in, they interviewed her, and released her back to us. They came out, lectured us, and said she was fine: "Take her home." I thought she might kill us.

She finally stopped drinking after multiple stays in detox and rehab hospitalizations. Gratefully, she finally heard what she needed to hear, although unfortunately it was after she lit the couch and the house on fire when she passed out with a cigarette. We lost the entire contents of the house but the house itself didn't burn down. Emotionally, we were all done with her at that point. Somehow, on her resulting rehab admission, she heard what she had to hear. She had 20 years of sobriety following that event and was one of my best friends—what a gift.

During my teenage years, my older brothers and sisters were busy with their own lives. They had all moved out and moved on. Why wouldn't they? That was exactly what they were supposed to do. There was only one problem: it left two of us at home. Those were the dark years—and it's when grace started actively searching for me.

I was never physically hurt. I just felt invisible, never seen or heard. I used to walk around in life with three questions that I still carry with me:

Does anyone know I am alive?

What is my purpose here?

Do I matter?

Those are the voices of self-doubt that I still hear to this day.

Little did I know that these questions would become the focus of my adult life as a coach because I discovered we all have to tackle these questions at some time.

You may have grown up in a home that did not resemble Beaver Cleaver's home or, in other words, a perfect household. You may have been through some really hard things or are in the middle of them now. You may have been dealt some hard circumstances or, due to your own decisions, you have contributed to your struggles.

Or you may actually have a good life and you know it could be better...

In this book I aim to share with you 5 steps you can take, no matter where you are, to help you to move forward and make the best of each moment and each day. You know when they add up—it's your life, and you are worth it.

Introduction
Cracking the Grace Code

If you are anything like me, you want to live your best life and you are willing to do what you can to get there. You have tried many things and you're tired of people telling you lame ways to improve your life. Grace Trail Process has been my work for over a decade and it can help you to make strides toward inviting grace into your life in ways you never imagined possible. I know this because that is what people tell me when they *walk the trail.*

As a professional life coach for the past 15 years, I have had the honor of working with thousands of people in hospitals, corporations, camps, corporate and personal retreats, and regular people like you and me who need to find their footing in this crazy world to move forward in the right direction.

Through my own life challenges and my work with others, I have found a unique process that includes 5 Grace Trail questions. These are the essence of what we need to access to move through the confusion of any life situation to a better place.

I wrote this book to make Grace Trail accessible to anyone—anywhere, anytime—who wants to shine some light on their next step and ultimately the wisdom within them.

What I Know About Grace

How curious that I chose to write about something that is so difficult for me to define.

Although the definition eluded me earlier in my life, I knew I needed grace, desperately. I wanted to live in this world sanely and yearned for those precious moments, to just notice, make some choices, and let life unroll as it may.

> Every day you choose to center yourself
> in sanity or insanity.
> The difference is a little space.

Grace is here—somewhere, sometimes. You can't force it to show up, you can't always see it, and you had better be ready when it does show up because it doesn't hang around waiting for you. When it's not visible, it goes to the same place a good thought goes when ignored, misunderstood, or forgotten. You can't quite call it up again like with a remote for instant replay on TV.

I wish there was a switch, like a light switch, to click on to make good things happen—love, compassion, generosity, fun. You can set it all up but there are no guarantees any of it will show up.

That's what grace is like.

How would you explain or describe enthusiasm? Where is it in your body? How do you describe what a thought is and what it looks and feels like? How about laughter? How is it so contagious to everyone else around you?

What is all of that? How do all those things happen? Where do they go when they are done and not here anymore? Everyone would use different words and feelings to describe these things as we all value and experience them uniquely.

That's what grace is like.

It is sort of like the chemistry between actors that makes for a blockbuster movie. The script can be the same for other actors but the energy and outcome varies. You can't force that or predict it. The equation would look like $1 + 1 = 4$.

That's what grace is like.

I've worked the last decade trying to figure this out, trying to crack the grace code. I still don't have the answer and that is the grace code. I still don't have the answer and that is the mystery and wonder of grace.

You don't *have* to have the answer to understand grace. You can be the answer by living your life with curiosity, compassion, and courage. Good questions can help you to get there.

What is Grace?

Grace is a gift from the universe or God or source or your angels or higher power or whatever being, concept, or phrase you use to understand your world in a meaningful way. It is a gracious and active communication of a gift that is free of any claim or judgment about you being worthy enough or needing to pay it back. You can't buy it or make it happen.

Some people don't acknowledge it, don't believe it exists, or have a narrow definition of what they think it is. Others feel you must be religious to receive it. I am not here to argue the definition or convince you of anything. You've got to want to understand to get it.

I believe grace is available to everyone who chooses to open their head, heart, and soul to the possibility of it showing up in their life. As each of you *walk the trail* you will receive whatever your experience offers each time and each time it will be different. You need to be okay with that and patient as the trail will unfold exactly as it is meant to.

There are steps you can take to welcome grace into your life more often and that's what this book is about.

The Essence of Grace

- Grace matters.

- Grace is a gift received at unexpected, undeserved, unasked for times.

- Grace can provide the catalyst and nutrients for more good to happen.

- Grace gives hope and momentum to push through the difficult times.

- Grace can fill your heart with gratitude, joy, and other positive emotions.

- Grace connects you in a heart-to-heart way to others.

- Grace elevates your spirit, letting you know you are not alone.

- Grace feels personal, intimate, and just right for you in just that moment.

Lessons Learned From Grace

Grace is not always graceful... Sometimes, it can be downright messy.

I had to go through some really difficult times to understand that:

> *Life is precious.*
> *Life is short.*
> *Life is tough.*

Now, I get it. Don't get me wrong. I don't claim the corner on pain and suffering. I don't want that corner. I have wonderful things going on in my life and actually my life is pretty darn good. But the truth is that I did not always grasp those three truths. I took life, my health, and vitality for granted. I was in my 30s when I was diagnosed with melanoma and I remember saying to the doctor, "I am only 32! How can I have cancer?"

When my husband was diagnosed with adrenal cancer. I thought, "What?! He never gets sick! How can he have cancer?" That wasn't supposed to happen. That wasn't in my plan.

Most of my life I thought my parents would be around forever. They were the pillars that were holding my future steady and keeping me young, as they were always older. When they passed, I felt like I had moved toward my own mortality.

I needed a few cataclysmic life shocks to really get those three lessons and that is the grace from the mess. I get it now...

Life is precious. Life is short. Life is tough.

I try to live each day holding those truths by savoring the good, sharing the good, and inviting more of it.

Life is Precious, Grace Matters

I know Grace matters because it saved my life. I was never in danger of ending my life but during a particularly difficult period—my parents were dying, I had teenagers, and I was changing professions—my light felt like it was going out, like the last embers of a campfire. When I first discovered the Grace questions, it was like putting kindling on the fire, blowing gently, and seeing the slight glow appear and sparks fly.

It was the hope of a blaze that got me on my feet and looking for sticks for the fire. As I asked the Grace questions, and my husband joined me, a small flame would occasionally appear, just a flicker at first.

The questions fed the fire—my desire—my energy to go forward.

In the beginning, asking those questions felt like hard work, like bringing the logs back to the fire. The answers were not always easy and often brought up memories and feelings I didn't want to look at, hear, or feel.

It felt very out of control to be studying as a life coach while assisting (with the help of all my siblings) my parents to pass away. No matter what we did, they got weaker. At the same time, I was a life coach who did not have the answers for her struggling teens.

After a while, I sidled up to those questions and got to know them well. I became more comfortable both with not knowing the answers and being near some uncomfortable things that brought me pain. For me, that was the way through.

The Grace in the mess is that over time I got the twinkle back in my eyes and the bounce back in my step.

The Grace questions helped me to fan the flames of hope—hope that we could get through to a better place, inch by inch, question by question, step by step.

Life Can Change In a Moment

It was shocking when my husband received a diagnosis of adrenal cancer. There was a cancerous tumor on his adrenal gland, forcing the gland to excrete extremely high amounts of adrenaline that could kill him. While in the hospital waiting for surgery, we were visited by the cardiologist who informed us that the surgery was extremely dangerous and that we should "get your affairs in order." Translation: he may not make it through the surgery.

We got on the phone and contacted everyone who could help us "get our affairs in order" and then we cried, prayed, and reached out to family and friends.

After we did everything in our control to get things in order, we started walking the hospital halls—my husband with a heart monitor taped to his chest and pushing an IV pole. We started asking and answering the five questions. I didn't know it then but we were walking Grace Trail—walking the trail to manage our fears and help us to walk back into hope. We needed that before the surgery to manage our emotions as we focused on what was within our control.

Gratefully, my husband made it through and is healthy today, many years later.

Life is Short, Hope Matters

The longer I live, the faster it seems to go. The better I get at navigating life challenges, the more challenges I seem to get. The days now seem to go by in 5 minutes and weeks seem like a day and that is why the ability to access hope matters so much.

I feel an urgency to maximize my short time on earth. Hope helps us all to do this. Grace Trail helps you to access hope when you are in darkness. It is like the hinge on a door that swings open just enough to light your way.

Hope keeps our eyes focusing ahead on where we want to go and what we want to create. A belief that tomorrow will be better helps you to move forward, sustain your energy, and access more as you overcome obstacles. Hope searches for pathways to get us to that desired future.

I have been a professional life coach for 15 years and have helped thousands of people to transform the way they live and work. I go into businesses and share this information to help people to thrive in challenging workplaces. When you get right down to it, one of the most important things that I do as a coach is to help people access hope. It can move mountains, cure horrible diseases, and win some fierce battles. And from there, so much more is possible.

I also try to spread hope wherever I go. In the process of needing to tell people about Grace Trail and the work I am doing, I have created some novel ways to share some novel ideas. I began to collect small beach stones and write inspirational words on one side and GraceTrail.com on the other. I use them as a kind of business card. However, they are so much fun to give out that I typically keep a couple of rocks in my pocket and just notice people who may wander into my path during the day. If it strikes me that they need a smile or if their smile is radiant, I give them a "smile" stone. Sometimes I just smile and say, "Here is my business card" as I hand them a stone. They always smile at that. Other times, I just hand the stone to them. It is amazing to see the skepticism on some people's faces initially when I try to hand them something. In that case I say, "It is free and it won't hurt you." Then they reach out, take it, read it, and smile. I may say, "You have a great smile." Or I might just say, "Enjoy."

I also leave what I call "message" rocks wherever I go—beach stones that I write on. Some of the messages that I scatter are Hope, Joy, Courage, Gratitude, and Grace.

I believe that whoever needs that message is the one who will find it. Those stones always disappear quickly.

Grace Can Be as Simple as a Smile

I have shopped at the same food store for years. The store is quirky and fun and the employees are always in a good mood for their customers—they really work it.

I've gotten to know the employees well from chatting over the years. I noticed one of my store employee "friends" was not looking well over the previous weeks. He is someone who always chats and we check in on the latest news, weather, and just general light, life stuff. I could tell by his silence and the look on his face that something was really wrong. I gently inquired and he very briefly and seriously said he was not well and needed some sort of treatments. I knew he didn't want to say more and he didn't have to. I reached in my pocket and said, "Do you need one of these?" I gave him a beach stone with SMILE written on it. He said, "Yes, I do need one of these. Thanks." He gave the hint of a smile, put it in his pocket, and walked away.

I forgot about that stone.

About 6 months later, I randomly decided to leave a stone with the word HOPE written on it in the same store at one of the checkout cash registers, in the little rack holding the mints and gum. Yes, it is a strange hobby but I like to think I could be doing a lot worse.

And there I left it, HOPE, nestled into the products, for anyone to see, pick up, and put in their pocket.
I forgot about that stone.

About a week later, I was shopping and my store "friend" came up to me and said, "Were you here yesterday?"

"No," I replied. "I was here about 5 days ago."

"Well, I was cleaning up yesterday around one of the registers and I found one of your HOPE stones. But 5 days ago? Do you know how many hundreds of people passed that stone until I found it? I knew you left it there for me."

He said, "I took it home and put it on the window sill beside my SMILE stone. My roommate saw it and said, 'Oh look! First you got your Smile and then you got your Hope.'"

I think that is how a smile and hope can work together; although, sometimes, first you get some hope and then you get a smile.

Life is Tough, Resiliency Matters

When I think about the fact that *life is tough*, there is a fine line between being bitter and angry and just being ready. I want to be nimble on my feet as I take the lessons from life as wisdom and not a heavy, hardened shell of protection.

Challenges and struggles don't seem to get dealt out evenly as many seem to get more than their fair share. Do you ever notice life challenges come in waves, one after another? I know that is happening when I hear myself saying, "They just need a break."

That is why resiliency matters so much. We certainly strive to and must survive our challenges but our next goal has to be to come out stronger on the other side and use the knowledge gained to adapt. We don't have enough time on earth to keep repeating the same mistakes again and again.

As I get older, the challenges somehow seem to get bigger. What I have noticed in my life is, the bigger the challenge the more courage is required of me. I have found the need to call on my courage frequently. I found the need to make up a new word to add to the English language describing my state of being when called on to be most courageous—when both scared and courageous at the same time.

The new word is: **s'courageous**©

Instead of letting the fear decide for me, I let it inform me. Often I can't wait until the fear subsides to take some courageous actions. I work to acknowledge it as I make decisions—the bigger the risk, the bigger the fear, the more courage needed. Courageous moments are when we choose to go forward in our life despite fear, negative thoughts, or any guarantees about the outcome because we know, in our heart, that it is the right thing to do.

What Grace Knows About Me

The more curious I am about Grace, the more I learn and the more I realize I don't know. It is in this space of not knowing, of letting go of the need to know, that Grace shows its lovely face.

Grace reminds me that there are forces invisible to me that are working behind the scenes on behalf of myself and others. It reminds me that I am not alone and I am not the one calling the shots—which is different from having choices, initiating action, and taking full responsibility.

Grace encourages me to have faith, which at times, is not easy.

I have the welcome mat out for Grace anytime and anywhere it decides to show up. I am not counting on its arrival or even expecting it, but patiently staying open to the possibility.

But I will not just sit idle. I am encouraging Grace with good will, my best intentions and efforts, and sharing it when it arrives, savoring the glow from that gift for as long as it is possible.

Grace and hope walk hand in hand with me toward living a more vibrant and resilient life. I know this is available for you, too.

Every day you choose to center yourself
in sanity or insanity.
The difference is a little **grace**.

...and now let's go to the steps.

Part I

What is Grace Trail?

Where the adventure begins...

Chapter 1
How It All Happened

It is only when you get to the other side of tough times that you can, hopefully, see the value and appreciate it—or at least appreciate parts of it. As life throws chaos and challenges at you, it is hopefully then that you work to try and bring order back to your life and figure it out. The chaos brings new information and options that we may not have seen or be willing to try when life is all neat and ordered. Some people seem to get on the life track that seems like "life as usual." My life seems to have taken the track, "Life as unusual." I like that framework better as life doesn't seem to catch me off guard so much when it throws me one of those curve balls.

I am going to put the timeline together for you for how this all happened. Grace Trail has evolved over fifteen years. This chapter will begin when Grace Trail was created when my son was in Afghanistan in 2012. However, the concept of the 5 steps of Grace and the 5 questions have been growing since my family hit some really hard times in our home and I attempted to figure it out, 15 years ago.

Afghanistan 2012

My son was a soldier serving in combat in Afghanistan, and I was a mother struggling with my fears back here at home. I would lay in bed thinking about what he and his unit must be coping with. His job was to search for IEDs or bombs buried in the road—a job that constantly put him in danger of being blown up by explosives and by enemy fire. I found myself waking in the middle of the night in a panic, knowing there was nothing I could do. Sometimes talking to him while he was there was almost worse. The reality of his situation was burned in my mind.

People would always ask about my son and after that they would say, "How do you do it?" I didn't have an answer for that. What were the choices?

The Army offered Resiliency Training for families who had loved ones in combat. They talked about the challenges of the soldiers returning home to the "new normal."

It got me thinking...

"How does someone walk from those battlefields to living life here again?"

"How do they access hope after that and put all that behind them?"

"How do I?"

During my son's deployment, I read an article about a town in Maine through which the Appalachian Trail passes. This town's economy largely relies on tourism and Trail hikers.

In the article, someone was asked, "Who are the people that are hiking the trail?" The reply was, **"It is a lot of vets *walking off their war.*"**

Wow! Walking off their war. That image really hit me.

I asked myself, "Where can I go to *walk off my war?*"

I can't easily get to the Appalachian Trail as that runs from Georgia to Maine and I can't easily get to the Pacific Crest Trail, which runs the length of California, Oregon, and Washington. Those trails run for thousands of miles and take months to hike. I did not have that in mind. I needed something shorter and more accessible so I could walk it whenever I needed it. So I started to imagine a trail where someone could "walk off their war"—without straying too far from home.

I started thinking, what if people came to a spot on earth that inspires and elevates them and, then at that point, ask themselves some simple questions? How would the answers be different? What new perspectives could be accessed as they look within themselves from this point?

That was when I created a trail in my hometown of Plymouth, MA, and I call it Grace Trail. Since the creation of the Grace Trail, hundreds, maybe thousands, of people have walked it. This trail—really, just a suggested route—is about a mile long and meanders past a harbor, onto a rocky beach, through a beautiful field, and down a little hill. This all takes place on land and trails that people are already allowed and encouraged to walk on. I made the trail as unobtrusive as possible by nestling natural beach stones into the landscape. I invited people in their wandering to organically find the trail by just being curious.

I tied these questions and the idea of a trail together in my mind as I noticed the impact the walking trail had on me and others I walked with. I decided to paint the letters of Grace on some large beach stones and place these stones along a path—the path that I now call Grace Trail.

My goal was for the trail to elevate people's spirits and open their minds and hearts. Let the trail comfort, confront, or confound—meet them wherever they are. The questions will take them wherever they need and want to go. I know this because the trail does all of that for me.

When Grace Found Me

For over a decade, long before the creation of the trail, I had been working with the idea and concept of Grace. It wasn't until I put it on a trail and a map that people really got what it was all about. This physical manifestation of the Grace Trail Process put it within people's reach, off the paper and into their world.

Though my married family and I have had some wonderful times and wonderful years together, it has not always been easy. We have been through some tough times, with one particularly difficult stretch more 10 years ago. I found myself married with children sandwiched between the needs of my aging parents. Both of my parents were dying and passed away within 6 months of each other. I have five siblings and on most days there were not enough of us to do all that needed to be done. There was a time when my Dad was in five medical facilities in 6 weeks, and then my mother passed away on one floor of the hospital while my father was having surgery two floors up. It was daunting.

At the same time, my two children were teenagers and we found these years to be very trying. Both my children were "creative and challenging" teens, but in very different ways. We had lots going on with medical and school issues, behavior challenges, and just plain old teenage stuff. I would run between different facilities trying to support my parents while juggling all that was going on at home. It felt like there was no break from all of this—no time to recover.

During this time, I was also making a career change, returning to school to become a professional life coach. This school required many hours in the classroom with experiential learning and a certification period that took about two years total to complete. I had practiced as an occupational therapist for a decade and then went into various businesses after getting my MBA. Becoming a coach was one of the most natural changes I have ever made. I felt like I finally found my place and I think I have always been a coach at heart. But, doing this during this particular time, where any one of those struggles alone would have been enough, together they stunned me. It felt like waves during a storm knocking us over, again and again.

I lost my balance, my breath, and my bounce—but I still had a lot to do, still had to function, somehow. I found myself saying, "I have to step into a state of grace." I wasn't even sure what that meant but I knew it was a lot better than where I was.

I felt there must be a quieter place right next to me but I couldn't seem to find my way there. I was looking for the "eye in the middle of the storm"—a way to continue to function and move ahead in the midst of the chaos. Confused and weary, I was looking for a plan, some hope.

I didn't understand it then (and I am not sure now I understand how it happened), but that was when I found Grace, or more accurately, when Grace found me. I can still remember the moment when I saw these five words in my head:

Gratitude

Release

Acceptance

Challenge

Embrace

And I started asking five important questions:

Even though life is hard, ***What am I grateful for?***

Even though I carry burdens, ***What can I release? Let go of?***

Even though I feel confused, ***What is calling out for acceptance?***

Even though I am overwhelmed, ***What is my next challenge?***

Even though I feel unsure, ***What can I embrace as possible?***

I found that as I asked myself these questions and listened for the answers, it was as if I was walking from fear and tightness toward hope and possibility, and I felt relief each time.

I would call my husband at work and have him listen as I asked and answered the questions. He is a busy pediatrician who did not really have the time to listen to me, but, gratefully, he never said no. These calls usually just took a couple of minutes to run through, and then one night, he came home from work and said, *"Let's do Grace together."*

That was when we started walking around the block every night after work for an entire summer, asking those questions and listening to each other's answers. Each night we got different answers. My husband will tell you it greatly supported our marriage and I will tell you it radically changed my life. We also realized that it was the first time all day that anyone had really listened to us, and it was the first time we got to say honestly what we were feeling and experiencing. We found a connection to each other during a really scary time.

I didn't know it then but we were walking the Grace Trail and we have never stopped walking it together.

Each of the struggles in my life was very different and together, they were overwhelming. Each time I asked the questions, even just one of questions, it helped me to clarify each situation and moment a little more. It helped me to find some ground to pause and find my footing so I could proceed with a little more assurance that I was moving in the right direction.

This was the beginning of something wonderful that began and evolved from pain.

...and that was how it all began.

Chapter 2

The Original Grace Trail and Map

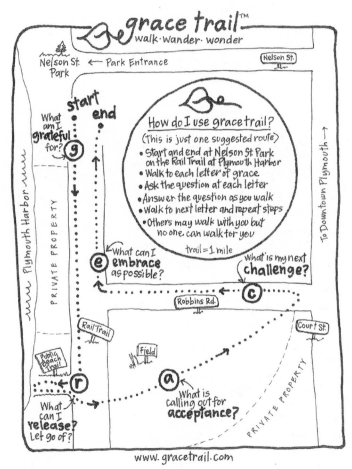

grace trail™
walk · wander · wonder

Nelson St. Park ← Park Entrance   Nelson St.

start end

What am I **grateful** for? (g)

How do I use grace trail?

(This is just one suggested route)

- Start and end at Nelson St Park on the Rail Trail at Plymouth Harbor
- Walk to each letter of grace
- Ask the question at each letter
- Answer the question as you walk
- Walk to next letter and repeat steps
- Others may walk with you but no one can walk for you

trail = 1 mile

To Downtown Plymouth →

Plymouth Harbor

PRIVATE PROPERTY

What can I **embrace** as possible? (e)

What is my next **challenge?** (c)

Robbins Rd.

Rail Trail

Court St.

Field

Public Beach Trail

(r)

(a) What is calling out for **acceptance?**

What can I **release?** Let go of?

PRIVATE PROPERTY

www.gracetrail.com

artwork by Jill Powell

In this chapter, not only am I sharing the original map and suggested route but I am sharing other people's stories about their experience walking the trail. I hope you feel the enthusiasm that the trail brings to other's lives and, hopefully, envision it in your life. The 5 questions guide your experience no matter where you walk this trail. People are being creative and blazing their own trails all over the country—in back yards, offices, kitchens, and any other place where clarity in life is being called for. I hope the nutrients are here to feed your creativity so you can bring this into your world in whatever way works for you.

Hallowed Ground

As I was designing the path that Grace Trail would follow, it was important that I match the territory of the question with the geography of the land. By that I mean, I designed the trail to help answer those questions not only with your heart, but with the view and immediate surroundings.

When asking, "What am I grateful for?" you are at a spot on Grace Trail where it is so beautiful that you can't help but feel gratitude. If you can't find any other reason in your life to be grateful, be grateful for being right there. The trail helps you to experience the energy of gratitude flowing from your heart.

The Release stone brings you to a rocky beach where I envision people throwing rocks into the water as they answer the question: "What do I need to let go of?" The physical act of throwing rocks into the water helps you feel your way to answers as you experience what true release feels like—the relief of letting go.

Acceptance finds you walking through a beautiful field of grass which I call the Field of Loving Awareness. I encourage people to be quiet in the field and listen as they ask themselves, "What needs to be seen and heard in my life?" Or "What do I need to accept?"

Challenge finds us walking downhill on a quiet road. As the pace picks up and the gentle steps become more like a march, you can feel the invigorating energy as you ask, "What is my next challenge?"

From there we complete the circle and turn onto the same beautiful part of the trail where we experienced gratitude as we inquire, "What can I embrace as possible?" This comes at the end of the trail, which has readied you to ponder the possibilities in your life.

Grace Trail meets you right where you are. It totally accepts you right where you are and lets you explore there with no expectation other than that. You invite yourself into a conversation about all that really matters to you.

Here is what one Grace Trail walker had to say about walking the trail:

It reminded me that big life changes are often best achieved with a series of smaller steps. We are meant to reflect in order to move forward with confidence. In a world that places so much value on instant gratification, it was wonderful to experience an actual path that encouraged me to slow down, walk through each emotion, fear, or doubt before I cross the finish line to the next phase. It reminded me that life is a journey and to value the transitional steps.

—M.S.

Someone Walking Their Grace Trail in Their Kitchen

It all started after I took a car ride with Anne. She had a few Grace Trail stones in her car and she shared an "accept" stone with me. I remember thinking that I did not want that one as I was trying to move through a relationship gone bad. For quite some time I had been kicking my feet and wanting things to be different, avoiding acceptance at all costs. That little stone helped to bring me to a new awareness. I could remain stuck or move on with acceptance. Acceptance allowed me to let go and gave me back a sense of freedom. The timing of that little stone was a true gift for me. Funny how life works.

Using the Grace Trail is so simple. It can be done anywhere, in my bedroom, back yard, or just in my head. I can do it with others or alone. It truly is a simple way to bring clarity to any challenge I am facing.

My stones sit on my windowsill in my kitchen where I seem to spend a lot of my time...they are a gentle reminder helping me to move through my challenges in a very practical helpful way!

–Therese Heney, DC

Adventure Starts with Questions

The five concepts are presented as questions because a question can be the beginning of a great adventure. Questions bring you beyond what you already know. They help you to be a learner in your own life and encourage you to approach situations, even very familiar ones, with a fresh perspective. These questions become like a guide post to direct your thoughts and emotions to what is strong and true. The secret to life is not having all the right answers, but more about asking the right questions. Curiosity will lead to pathways never before noticed, walked, or even in existence. Continuing to ask and answer these questions leads to subtle changes that add up to transformation over time.

These questions begin a dialogue around hope, resiliency, and grace instead of fear or doubt. They provide a catalyst for moving forward bringing freshness and clarity to any moment, situation, or challenge.

This is what I have heard from others walking the Grace Trail:

"Simple questions, not so simple answers."

"Now I have to be really honest with myself."

"This means I have to be honest with others..."

And my reply to them is, "That's okay. You'll make it through and you will make it through to a better place."

The more you ask, the easier it gets. As this becomes more of a habit, you begin to rewire your brain to search for these answers even when you are not asking the questions.

You may not get through all the questions at once and that's okay. Start anywhere. The important thing is to start asking and to listen with more than just your ears. You will ask what needs to be answered and somehow these questions will take you where you need to go when you are ready to go there. However, sometimes these questions take you where you need to go before you believe you are ready and that's where courage comes in.

Courage is a curious thing. Sometimes I find situations where I am unflinchingly brave, no hesitation, and then there are those times, that I really need to push myself forward. Being courageous can be just as risky as not being courageous and not acting. I find it is worth it to give it some thought and decide when it is best to muster your courage and walk forward.

Grace Trail questions encourage more than just a conversation as you walk and talk toward the life you wish to create. When you become an active partner in the process, committed to showing up in your life courageously, you walk the trail back to the best of you. No one can walk it for you.

Invite yourself out for a walk on Grace Trail, actually or virtually, where you walk, wander and wonder yourself to a better place. No matter where you are, each conversation begins with curiosity. I hope compassion and courage join you there and then you will be in the company of your best self.

Grace Trail provides access to your inner wisdom in a simple, honest way that is easy to remember, understand, and use. Don't complicate it. Don't overanalyze. Just walk it, talk it, ask it, and listen. You may not get through all the questions, but the important thing is to just start.

Walking the Trail

Grace is life, grace has life, and I now believe that grace has legs because it so frequently joins me walking the trail. Sometimes it jogs ahead and then waits for me and, other times, it stops me in my tracks. Take your heart for a walk and let your feet follow.

Walking stimulates the movement and energy of grace. Movement helps to push anxiety and excess energy out of your body and invites in calmness, helps to access your vitality, so you are refreshed, vibrant, and more creative. Energy shifts occur allowing emotions to flow. You step into a natural rhythm within yourself as you synchronize your thoughts and feelings. Though walking enhances the Grace Trail Process exponentially, it is not essential.

When you walk outside, all your senses are engaged. As nature and life surround you, it can feed you and positively affect you in many ways.

Moving forward under your own power, empowers you. The brain starts to go with your feet, ties in your heart, and things unfold in unexpected ways.

You can walk almost anywhere—it is free and nothing is needed but a safe place and your commitment. Leave a pair of sneakers in your car, at work, and at home. Make it happen—that may be your biggest challenge.

There are actual, physical Grace Trails and there are virtual Grace Trails. Walking enhances this process exponentially but it is not essential.

You can walk the Grace Trail in your mind, virtually—at your desk, during your commute, sitting quietly waiting your turn somewhere, or over coffee with a friend. This Grace Trail Process can be done alone, in pairs, or in groups. Though it is encouraged to ask and walk the questions in order, it is not required. These questions build on each other as they move you in a forward direction toward the life that you wish to create. At times, this may mean you do not know your exact destination but hopefully you are heading in the right direction. I lovingly call this floundering forward and highly recommend it as you live your life in a process of discovery.

More than One Trail

I made a map of the Grace Trail available on my website, for people to print or to view on their phone while walking, and I left maps around town in Grace Trail-friendly businesses. When the large beach stones with GRACE letters on them were repeatedly stolen from the trail, I decided to leave smaller stones for people to take with them. I printed inspirational words on small beach stones and left them at each station. It was only after I noticed people's enthusiasm when receiving these stones that I began giving them out to people in my travels. I ask people on the Trail to take just one and, happily, the larger stones stopped disappearing. These are serendipitous gifts that you may be fortunate enough to find. I also leave message stones hidden along the trail—be kind, joy, inspire yourself, be compassionate to you, hope, and smile are just a few reminders that you may happen to find.

Well, people found the Trail and people got it. I started hearing stories about the Trail from people who didn't know that I was The Grace Trail Lady. The Trail is over a year old as I write this. It has been embraced even by those who can't walk the actual Trail in Plymouth—these people are on their own unique trail, that they built themselves. Here are some stories of how some are making their own Grace Trails, right in their own backyards.

Grace Trail Came Into My Life

The Grace Trail gracefully came into my life recently and at a time carefully chosen by the universe. It was the beginning of gardening season and the Grace Trail has found a place among the lilies, hydrangeas, and begonias. Each year, I design my garden with no true design. It just organically calls out for what it needs and I do my best to understand the call and select flowers, plants, rocks, and other eclectic items. This year it also called out for the Grace Trail and I added ceramic birds each representing one of the Grace letters. I walk the trail watering the garden and asking myself the Grace Trail questions, opening my heart to the answers so truth can come in and awakening can occur. The walk reminds me that miraculous things occur and God answers if I really listen. "What is a moment that required me to be courageous and I was? How did I show courage? How does that moment make me feel grateful?" The garden dies in the fall like it always does...its season is over, but the Grace Trail does not. My birds will come inside for the winter and be put in a place where I can see them so they can continue to take me to a place of discovery, reflection, and of course . . . grace.

–Karen Senteio, VERVE LLC, Consulting Services

The Healing Power of Grace

I had heard Anne share the Grace Trail and the meaning of the acronym—I could see how people could embrace this and get a sense of peace or a next step, but I myself was not "practicing" the precepts of the Grace Trail. I was setting myself "outside" of the force field of the Grace Trail! My experience of the Grace Trail became personal when I accepted a professional work assignment that excited me and felt like a fit and a wonderful stretch—all after having reinvigorated my career post a mid-career break by working part-time. After 7 years of rebuilding a full-time career, I accepted a full-time position. The job was significantly more hours than expected with a different focus than laid out in the interview.

In managing the ensuing stress, I, with the support of my family, built a model of Anne's Grace Trail in my front yard. Every day I would walk my Grace Trail (north!) and often could only get through G—what am I grateful for, what am I grateful for. The Grace Trail was one of my sanctuaries even just working

38

the power of "G" to move from feeling stuck in my career to flow, addressing what were the key next steps to get my career back on track and make critical decisions, put the burden down of needing to stay stuck, and beginning to dip into "R." With Anne's help and my Grace Trail in my yard, I made the decisions I needed to make. My beautiful Grace Trail, Anne's support, and her concept of the Grace Trail were all part of the next steps' journey. Now I can move beyond G and regularly access the full power of Grace, of each step of each letter of the word. Happily, this summer my husband and I walked the Grace Trail in Plymouth with Anne and her husband—a wonderful conclusion to the healing power of Grace and my right next career steps.

–Karen J. Burke, Engineer, Executive Coach

Chapter 3

The Virtual Grace Trail and Map

The essence of Grace Trail can be captured without walking on an actual Grace Trail, or even walking at all. People are taking the questions with them and blazing their own trails as they go along, wherever they may be.

You can walk Grace Trail in your mind without lifting a foot.

These are the virtual trails that I refer to that make it possible to walk the trail anywhere, anytime, with anyone.

I encourage you to find physical locations that are accessible to you that calm you, feed your energy, connect you to your best or make your heart sing. Get yourself to those places often and let their energy elevate your spirit as you ask the Grace questions and listen for your answers. If possible, get walking; if that's not possible then sit, immerse yourself in the experience, and open yourself to receive the benefit.

On the following page is the map to walk Grace Trail anywhere, anytime, with anyone.

Grace Trail™ *by Anne Jolles*
walk... wander... wonder...

Walk It Anywhere, Any Time......Alone or With A Friend
Ask The Question... Listen For The Answer

You can walk while you ask the question and listen for the answer
Or just write your answers in a journal
Or just pause in your day and ask the questions.

Grace Trail™ Map

Start Here
Wherever you are...

End Here
Wherever you are...

Be Curious, Be Compassionate, Be Honest.
Listen for the answers.

With a Friend? Take turns answering,
Listen with an open heart,
No judgment, No advice.

Gratitude
What am I
grateful for?

Release
What do I need
to let go of?

Accept
What do I need to
accept in my life?

Challenge
What is my
challenge?

Embrace
What can I
embrace as
possible?

Gratitude... Release... Accept... Challenge... Embrace...

www. GraceTrail.com

Stories from the Virtual Grace Trail

Grace Trail in Big Bend, Texas

A couple of years ago, I ran into some significant relationship issues and my heart was broken. Filled with sadness, I tried to move on with my life. My friend Emily and I booked a trip to a National Park in Texas for the Fourth of July holiday weekend. As part of the trip, a park ranger recommended we hike the Lost Mine Trail and pointed us in that direction. I pulled out the Grace Trail map that Anne had shared with me and told Emily I would be walking the Lost Mine Trail as if it were the Grace Trail. She was completely on board with this idea and walked her own Grace Trail with me.

Here is what I discovered on this hike:

> *Gratitude–What am I grateful for? Loving family and friends like Emily who support me through this sad and difficult time. My health and the financial resources that made the trip possible.*

> *Release–What can I let go of? My anger at the recent events in my life—and, on that mountain, I screamed to release my angry and hurt feelings.*

> *Accept–What is calling out for me to accept? My sadness and inability to change the past. These feelings are valid and it's okay to feel this way.*

> *Challenge–What is the next challenge in my life? Graduate school. I will invest in myself and my future. Embrace–What can I embrace as possible? That I will*

find love again, and the right person to share my life with.

Grace Trail helped me more than I thought possible during one of the more trying times in my life. Now, it is not uncommon for me to go on a walk with these questions in mind. I share this story with others so that they, too, may experience the power of the Grace Trail.

–Chelsea Franklin

p.s. Gratefully, things have worked out really well and I am looking forward to the future.

Grace Trail to the Rescue

Super busy morning, rushing to get to my office by 8 AM, knew that I hadn't responded to the "must-do" e-messages...decided to take a few minutes to take a virtual walk on the Grace Trail.

Grateful–*that I am alive, healthy, and have so many things I'm interested in*

Release–*having to finish ten things before I go out the door*

Accept–*that I'm not superwoman*

Challenge–*choose one thing I can do now and let the others go*

Embrace–*that I can go out and cut some roses from my front yard to bring to my office.*

As I went out to the yard with my scissors, I was rushing a bit, but the sound of the garbage truck brought me to the "right-now" moment. On impulse, I waved to the guys. Decided to cut some roses for them.

Presto! When I handed over the first rose, the guy's face literally lit up. His eyes beamed, his smile showed missing two front teeth. His words? "This is the first time in 5 years that I've been given a rose by a doll!" Now I was smiling. To think that I almost missed that in my "must-do" rush.

Got to the office a few minutes late, more roses in hand.

And guess what? My 8 AM client was a no-show; she thought the appointment was for Thursday, not Tuesday.

Long live roses, time, space, garbage men, unexpected smiles— and the Grace Trail, even when it's virtual.

–Millie Grenough, Coach, Speaker, Author of *Oasis In The Overwhelm*, Clinical Instructor in Psychiatry, Yale University School of Medicine

grace trail®

5 Steps Toward Your Best Life

by Anne Jolles

G is for Gratitude:
What am I **grateful** for?

R is for Release:
What can I **release**? Let go of?

A is for Acceptance:
What is calling out for **acceptance**?

C is for Challenge:
What is my next **challenge**?

E is for Embrace:
What can I **embrace** as possible?

Chapter 4

Even though life has its challenges now...

What am I grateful for?

Imagine this...

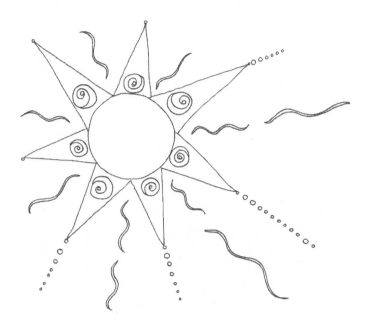

The sun shines warmly upon the earth, bringing the light and energy that is necessary for all of life, growth, and vitality. The seasons, climate, and weather depend on this amazing star that is at the heart of our solar system and the overarching energy source for all living things.

Where can I shine my light of appreciation today?

At this point on the Grace Trail in Plymouth, you would be in a space so beautiful that you could not help but to be grateful . . . to be just right there. You would be looking over a marsh to the harbor with boats, an island, and lots of sky. There is an osprey nest where you may be fortunate enough to see this family flying, nest building, and hunting for food.

The Essence of Gratitude

- Appreciation for what is going right in your life can lead to increased contentment and satisfaction.

- Sharing your gratitude with others enhances your positive feelings and your relationship with them.

- Gratitude will elevate you above the small details of your life.

- Operating from a perspective of gratitude can increase overall life satisfaction, which may positively change your perspective.

- Acknowledgment of what you appreciate in just this moment, or this day, will bring you into the present moment.

- Anticipation of events in the future that make you feel gratitude and joy will elevate your level of positive feelings.

- Cherishing good events in your past contributes to an elevated feeling of happiness.

- Gratitude brings you into the present moment. Joy lives in the present moment. Learning to stay in the here and now will increase opportunities for joy to enter your life.

- Gratitude ignites heartfelt energy that connects you to your heart and others' hearts.

- Gratitude is one of the few positive emotions that can be accessed from a feeling of fear or worry.

- Gratitude often leads the way toward hope.

Gratitude matters. There is a good reason that it is the first step on the Grace Trail. This is one of the steps that people love to take. It feels good as it connects you to what is good— and that alone has fantastic value. From there, the other steps become more reachable, tenable, and accessible as it lessens the resistance.

Gratitude is a sure-footed step toward grace that helps me to be present for more moments in my life. It is just like the sun, as an overarching energy source, as it feeds my health, vitality, and attitude. It connects me in a positive way in my relationships with those I really care about.

Joy can only enter your life when you are in the present moment. It cannot enter when you are worrying about the past, fretting about the future, and missing the present moment. Gratitude brings you into the present and can be accessed as easily as asking, "What am I grateful for?"

The Red Glass Heart

One of my family members is a single parent and at the time of this story she had two young children, ages 6 and 10 years old. After much contemplation and soul searching, she decided to move with her two children to the other side of the country in hope of building a life there. Our entire family got together for a party to send them off with good wishes. Besides giving them a little stash of "mad money," I was at a loss for what I could give them. I knew what a big step it was for them all. I had two little red glass hearts, small enough to fit in your hand, on my desk and I quickly grabbed them and gave one to each of the children. I told them to hold onto those hearts any time they needed to remind themselves of how much we all loved them. Both children silently put the heart in their pockets and left for the airport.

I forgot about those hearts.

Unfortunately, their adventure did not work out the way their mother had hoped it would and they moved back home abruptly, following a harsh and negative experience.

When the 6-year-old got off the plane, he walked up to his grandmother who was waiting for them, reached in his pocket and pulled out the red glass heart. He held it out to her and said, "I kept this in my pocket and held onto it every day."

We all need something to hold on to. We need to be able to hold onto what is good, what is strong, and what is true. That is what gratitude can do for you. Having gratitude is like keeping a little red glass heart in your pocket so you can reach in any time and remind yourself.

Gratitude takes the juicy and delicious parts of life and brings them front and center for you and others to enjoy over and over again. But you have to choose to use it. You have to reach in your pocket for that red glass heart or else it is just a piece of glass sitting there. Developing habits around gratitude and appreciation can impact your life in amazingly positive ways.

Holding onto and reminding ourselves of the good things is called savoring. There are so many different ways to savor, cherish, and remind ourselves of the positive.

Gratitude flows from your heart. We spend most of our day head-to-head connecting with others through working, problem-solving, thinking, and doing. Gratitude gets us out of our head and gets the energy flowing from our heart instead. It binds us to others with a heart-to-heart connection that ignites the energy from others' hearts. This is called heartfelt energy and it can move mountains. Heartfelt energy is what empowers your deepest drive toward meaning in your life.

Our heart is an amazing organ and it is so much more than just a pump for blood. Heartfelt energy is literally electric: your heart emits an electromagnetic field that changes when your emotions change. The heart is a vital connection between what you are feeling and what you are thinking, and how you are feeling affects those around you.

Gratitude is one of many positive emotions that helps us to be more creative and improves our ability to solve problems. Negative emotions have the opposite effect—creating chaos in our nervous system and making it hard to be present in our lives with vigor, enthusiasm, and creativity. It is impossible to be positive all the time and that's where Grace Trail works to walk you through your full range of moments and emotions. All emotions matter and can inform us.

The Oncology Nurse

During a workshop that I was running with cancer survivors, I asked each person to turn to the person sitting next to them and answer the following question, "Even though life may be very difficult right now, what am I grateful for?"

It really is quite a phenomenon, to give a presentation to a room of hundreds of people, and ask them to turn to the person next to them and answer that question. At first there is reluctance to begin but that always leads to difficulty in getting them to stop. This heartfelt energy has amazing power.

The energy in the room went through the ceiling as people took this time to focus on what was going right in their lives and, with their partner, cherish their appreciation in this moment. There was laughter and tears as all were welcomed and acknowledged.

An oncology nurse approached me quietly after the workshop and she was visibly upset. She said that she had no idea how to answer that question as there was absolutely nothing she could think of to be grateful for in her life.

Oy, no joy.

We are all very familiar with that negative downward spiral of emotion—so easy to trigger and fall down into. It becomes such a habit and a way of being that some of us live down there and don't even know it. The hard, negative things in life just seem to hang around longer than the positive, good ones which seem more fragile and short lived. However, we can learn to change our outlook so it tends to be more positive.

While negativity is contagious, the good news is that positivity is just as contagious. Gratitude can be the first step of initiating a positive upward spiral and inviting others to join you there.

Because the good parts of life seem so fleeting and to go by so fast, we have to learn to grab, cherish, and intensify them. Research tells us that for every tough situation we deal with, more positive ones are needed to balance the scales. This is where a conscious focusing on and savoring of what is going right brings about a tipping point toward positivity and all it has to give to us.

Past, Present, and Future

Gratitude is a very generous positive emotion. Not only does it speak a universal language, but you can access it and unleash its energy from all three perspectives of time—past, present, and future.

How can you savor some wonderful moments from the past?

You can place reminders of what you are grateful for in your path throughout your home and work. Photos, special letters, and other tangible items have meaning for you and remind you of the good in your life.

Each month, as I look ahead on my calendar and make some plans, I also look back at what I have accomplished in the past month. I put an accomplishments page right in my planner to remind me of all that has gone right. I tend to forget the successes and this helps me to savor those times.

How can you use gratitude to bring you into the present moment?

My pausing in the driveway that morning to notice and appreciate the situation allowed me to be present and to open my heart to the possibilities. Look at the joy in that moment.

Here is a way for you to appreciate the present moment:

SNAP! Out Of It!

> **S**top! and breathe…

> **N**otice! and breathe…

> **A**ppreciate! and breathe…

> **P**articipate! and breathe…

Just look around you, wherever you happen to be, and find something to appreciate and breathe it in!

You can do this four-step process while walking, sitting at your desk, on the subway—any place where you can pause your thoughts, look around, slow your breathing, and find something to appreciate.

Notice how your attitude and perspective change when you speak from the elevated feeling of gratitude.

How can you use gratitude to elevate your spirit for events in the future?

I expect many to read this and hopefully plan some moments of gratitude and joy for themselves or others that connect them from their heart to the world. The anticipation of Grace Trail making a positive impact in the future makes me grateful and gives me joy.

Take out your calendar and put yourself on it. Future planning brings joy from the research, planning, reaching out to others, and the actual anticipation of the pleasure.

The Language of Gratitude

Gratitude ... Glad About ... Generate More to Cherish ... Garner the best from the moment ... Graciously Moving Forward ... Giving Back

When my children were young, I wanted them to learn the language of gratitude so I would ask them, "What are you grateful for?" Eventually they got bored with it and they would roll their eyes and sigh which meant to me, "Not this gratitude stuff again." To appease me, my son began to give the same rote answer to the gratitude question, "All things good in the world." So I learned if I was going to talk the language of gratitude with my family, I was going to have to find some different words to engage them.

Here are some ways to enter a conversation about gratitude. I hope you adapt these ideas to fit your needs and style.

Glad about... What are you glad about?

Going right... What is going right today? at your job? in your life? in your relationship?

Gather good... How can you get more of that in your life? How can you gather more good and savor it?

Gifts... What are the gifts that you bring to a situation? What strengths did you bring to that situation for that positive outcome?

How did your efforts contribute to the success? What can you say to congratulate yourself?

Get greatest good from this moment... What else can you do to get the greatest good from this moment? How can you get more of that in your day? What would "even better" look like? How can I capture these good moments so I can be reminded of them?

Generate more... Now that you know what makes you feel grateful, how can you make more of that happen in your life? What would you do in your life to make it even 1 percent happier?
Give yourself the acknowledgment that you deserve and yearn for. How did your efforts contribute to the success? What can you say to congratulate yourself?

Generous to you: What can you plan in the future to enjoy yourself and others?

What made you laugh today?

Did anything inspire you today? Did you inspire anyone today?

Did you receive any kindness? Give any kindness? Observe any kindness?

Out of Gas

Early one sunny, spring Saturday morning, I took my dog Willie out for his first walk of the day. As I walked down the driveway I noticed a car with little kids in it parked in front of my house. A man was walking up the driveway next door and he said to the painter who was working on my neighbor's house, "Hey, I am out of gas. Can you help me?" The painter replied, "Sorry, I don't live here, I don't have any gas, and I don't have time to drive you anywhere."

Upon hearing this interchange, I realized I had a little gas in the garden shed for my lawn mower. So, Willie and I got the red gas can with just enough in it to get someone to a gas station. As I started walking back down my driveway with the gas can, I heard this out-of-gas guy talking on the phone. It sounded like he was in big trouble. I had sort of made up this story in my mind that he was divorced and he finally had the kids for his weekend and here he was... out of gas... again.

The conversation was going something like this, "Well, I am having a little problem. Nothing serious but I might be a little late with the kids." At this point, one of the children in the back seat saw me walking toward the car.

She shouted, "Dad! Look!" and pointed at me. The father glanced over and said, "Let me call you back."

I held out the can and said, "Here is some gas."

He said, "Oh thank you! Let me pay you."

I said, "I don't want any money."

He said, "Then let me use the gas and then fill it and bring it back."

I said, "I don't want any gas back. Just take it and get on with your day."

He said, "But, what do you want?"

I said, "I don't want anything. I'm glad to help. Do something nice for someone else. Leave the tank at the mail box and you're all set."

He took the can with one hand and took my other hand and squeezed it.

Willie and I continued our walk, later picking up the empty gas can waiting for me at my mailbox.

I didn't think about it again until the next weekend, when, as I was walking Willie on Saturday morning, I found this note and two pots of flowers:

Dear Stranger,

There is a shortage of three things in the world:

1. Kindness
2. Flowers
3. Gasoline

Thank you for helping me with #1 and #3.

S.

I saved that note and hung it on my refrigerator for a year to remind me and my family of a special moment. When people walked into the kitchen and were curious about the note, I would share that morning with them and enjoy again the feelings of that encounter.

This story played out using the language of the heart and while gratitude is its first language, many others live there— love, empathy, compassion, respect, generosity, forgiveness. The only thing required of you to join this conversation and learn this language is to rise above your own self-interest enough to share and celebrate the goodness within you with others and the world.

I heard the request for gas with my heart and the house painter, out of necessity, heard it from his head. The stranger gratefully responded with touch, flowers, a note, a smile, eye-to-eye contact, and a surprise. These are all the language of the heart. What a thank you! Each was received by my heart with joy and years later that act of giving and gratitude lives on to elevate your spirit in this book!

Our senses of touch, hearing, sight, smell and taste are wired to give and receive messages of gratitude. Sometimes in life words do not fully express what we feel. Our five senses can fill in for us to evoke the feeling when words are not enough. Our senses lay in wait for this. Don't make them wait too long.

Here are some ways the five senses both give and receive these messages of gratitude:

> **Auditory/ Hearing:** hear it, sing it, listen to songs and poetry

> **Touch:** hugs, handshake, gentle loving touch

> **Visual/sight:** thank you notes, gifts, signs, books, balloons

> **Smell:** flowers, comfort food

> **Taste:** bake a cake or a special dish for someone and enjoy

And then there is a wonderful and surprising sixth sense that our heart articulates with nonverbal senses. The sixth sense is the heart-to-heart connection you feel, the inner felt sense, that comes from within and can be shared and then felt by others. The heart has an electromagnetic field that radiates out and can be felt and actually measured many feet from the body. Our feelings of gratitude can positively impact others who happen to be nearby.

Research tells us that there are proven ways to savor the good and to elevate your spirit and attitude. To savor is to celebrate, cherish, and appreciate. There are ways to elongate the plea-surable moments in our lives for the experience of increased positive feelings. It is a way to turn our attention from the negative to the positive to focus on what is going right.

My life has just gone by too darn fast. I have more of my life behind me than ahead of me. I feel like one of the luckiest people in the world, determined to live as many moments of what gratefully remains.

I remember, after I had the melanoma removed from my back, recovering from the surgery and awaiting more results to determine if it had spread. Back then, thirty years ago, there was no treatment available for this. You either removed it all or you died. Friends came to visit me and had looks on their faces of fear and pity, like I was now in a different club than they were. I kept thinking the only difference between me and you is that I know my odds of survival and you just aren't aware of yours. Because, we are all going sometime. We seem in such a hurry and we miss so many moments looking everywhere except where we are right now.

I think that is why I enjoy being in the company of and work-ing with cancer survivors—or, to be really clear, survivors of anything. Survivors of life. They get it. The whole facade of you being in one club and me being in another is gone. They understand too well that Life is precious, Life is short, and Life is tough. We seem to get to what is really important fast-er. Not that we always have that and hold onto that in every moment but we seem to find our way back there sooner. May-be that's the gift from those hard times. There is a nod to what they are grateful for and what is really important because they have lost it all or almost lost it all.

There is so much to be learned from our hearts and I am committed to noticing and acknowledging life's gifts and benefits.

Gratitude gives us a break from this crazy world. Our brains release calming chemicals when experiencing these positive emotions and this gives our brains and bodies relief from the chemicals that are released in response to stress. The stress of everyday life uses high amounts of our energy. Using gratitude throughout your day can give you more energy and stepping into the present moment consumes less.

Gratitude reminds us that life exists inside—as well as outside—us all and it can connect you to an inner world just waiting to welcome you and join the other positive emotions within. Remember, though, these emotions need the oxygen of your attention to grow.

Do you need any more reasons to incorporate gratitude into your life?

Switchbacks to Access the Energy of Each Step

A **switchback** is a trail on a steep hill or mountain that is a zigzag pattern instead of a straight trail. This pattern protects the hill and the trail from excessive erosion. Trails that go straight up and down steep hills get excessively worn down.

So these switchbacks help you to zigzag your way on the Grace Trail and get out of those old ruts that block your vision and erode your vitality. They are meant to shake it up, ambush your boredom, surprise your nervous system, nourish your sense of adventure, and get you out of your comfort zone and out of your own way.

Choose one of the following to do whenever you want to infuse your day with more gratitude, then stand back and watch the change in you and your life.

- Put one hand over your heart. Feel it beating. Breathe. Now ask yourself, "What is going right in my life?" And listen to the answer and feel the answer.

- Or, find a partner who you trust and wish to connect with heart to heart. Do the above only, this time, put your hand on their heart and they put their hand on your heart. Feel it beating. Breathe. Now ask each other, "What is going right in your life?" And listen to the answer. Feel the energy of gratitude ignite as you look into each other's eyes.

- Do a self-hug: Wrap your arms around yourself and gently squeeze. Now ask your tired self, "What is one thing that I did right today?" Feel what it is like to be acknowledged and appreciated by you.

- Pay for the coffee for the person in line behind you at the drivethrough window and then drive away. Think of other small ways to pleasantly surprise a stranger or someone you know. Start small ripples of kindness that hopefully help to elevate the spirit of others through their gratitude. It can be contagious.

- Start every conversation today with, "What is going right?" You may not say those exact words but steer the conversation in that direction. Notice others' resistance when we shift to what is right instead of what is going wrong.

- Take out your calendar and plan an event that would give you pleasure to both plan, anticipate the arrival of that day and then enjoy. Elongate the pleasure of the event.

- Reach out to someone and acknowledge them and appreciate them for their efforts—not just their accomplishments or success, but for trying and not quitting even when it gets tough. Experience the heart felt energy of gratitude with others.

- Write that letter of appreciation. Who needs to hear from you that they made a difference in your day, your life, or someone else's? Feel that in your heart and notice the impact from that person's heart.

- Turn the corners of your mouth up and smile 10 times today even if at first you are faking it. Exercise those muscles! Watch the nonverbal reaction from others as you replace your scowl with a smile. Let yourself know that you are okay.

- Watch a movie or show that makes you laugh or inspires you. Experience this simple way to elevate your spirit and enjoy the benefits for hours following it.

- Watch a TED talk that inspires you every day for a month. Notice how your conversation with others evolves to start to incorporate some of what you learned, were inspired by, and felt.

- Give a hug to someone who really needs one. Feel the energy of gratitude.

- Call your mother, father, or the person who feels like a parent to you. If you can't think of anyone then reach out to someone whose relationship you would like to nurture. Connect from your heart.

- Turn off the news and the constant drone of fear and paranoia and get your update on the world in summary and smaller doses. Limit the drain.

- Congratulate yourself for something that you deserve to be recognized for. Do it now. Do it out loud. Do it daily. You can be your own bank account of goodwill.

- Get those old family, friend, or vacation videos digitized so you can remember the good times, often.

- Put some of your favorite photos and moments into picture frames so you can be reminded of the good times, often.

- Find a spot on earth that makes you feel alive and go there, often. Replenish.

- Stop giving to people who are not appreciative of your gifts. Cherish your value.

- Use the language of the heart to thank someone—so, not in words. Practice communicating with the language of the heart.

Questions to take with you on the Trail

1. What are three things I value about myself? How are they gifts to others? How can I strengthen them? How can I share them more often? Where do I need to set some limits and stop sharing?

2. Who do I wish to reach out to in a warm, positive way to let them know how much I appreciate them or their efforts or their accomplishment?

3. When I think back over the past 24 hours, what can I be grateful for? What if I end every day with this as my last thought?

4. What is something that I have done today that I wish to be acknowledged for? How can I congratulate myself for my success? My efforts?

5. What is going right in my life? My home? My work? My play?

Chapter 5

Even though I carry a heavy load...

What can I let go of?

Imagine this...

It is a sunny, cool autumn day in New England. Nature is in all of its brilliant glory as vibrantly colored leaves fall from the trees. The trees are left bare. This release is a necessary part of the preparation for winter where they will quietly rest and replenish. The falling leaves have cleared the way for new growth in the spring.

What do I need to make room for in my life?

At this point on the Grace Trail in Plymouth, you would be walking down a path toward the harbor and stepping onto a rocky beach. You could bend, pick up a stone, and throw it into the water as you experience the physical release of letting it go.

The Essence of Release

- Letting go releases life-altering energy that allows you to move forward, hopefully toward what you desire to create in your life.

- You must be clear on what it is you want and need to release before you can let it go.

- Holding onto people or events that prevent you from moving forward can block your view and taint your perspective.

- We often try to avoid the discomfort around letting go by denying, blaming, and distracting ourselves.

- When you are sure about what is holding you back then you can choose what you want to do about it and how you are going to do it.

- Fear and self-doubt often appear when you let go or consider letting go. It may appear easier to stay in discomfort or pain rather than step into the unknown.

- Release may take hard work, courage, and honesty.

- Conscious change can only happen when we make room in our lives for new things to enter.

- Sometimes we can be really clear on what we want to let go of and what we need to let go of—and it is just not the time for that to happen.

Accounts to Draw Upon

My husband and I were driving through the beautiful, rural backroads of Vermont.

"Stop the car!" I shouted. "What does that sign say?"

He pulled over and on the side of a huge silo, in a field next to a barn, was a sign written in big letters that read, "Manure Bank." We looked at each other in disbelief. What an intriguing concept—apparently manure matters around these parts.

My husband looked at me and said, "That thing sure can hold a lot of sh*t."

Steven Covey wrote the best-selling book, *Seven Habits of Highly Successful People*. I can still remember, 15 years later, his instruction in that book for improving relationships by building what he referred to as a "bank account of goodwill." He explained that as you put deposits of love and kindness into this account, a reserve of goodwill builds in the relationship that you can fall back upon and reach into when things hit a rough patch.

On Grace Trail, we have to access a different type of bank

account. In all of our lives, we have entire vaults of things we need to let go of—some of it quite messy. In letting go, we have to reach into a bank account but this is a different type than Covey wrote about. This one often resembles the silo that sat in the field in the pasture in Vermont.

Letting go is not always easy but your life depends on it. Your ability to know what to hold onto and what to let go of will determine your level of happiness and life satisfaction. Demands come at us at an increasing rate and intensity—we can't carry it all with us. Letting go is essential for us to be an active part of the process of change and creating the change that we desire.

The Grace Trail process helps you engage in change by increasing your awareness. Everything changes and we all seem to resist change . . . not always easy.

The only thing harder than letting go is trying to drag something along that needs to be released. It often takes courage and compassion to let go.

The Gymnast

My daughter is a gymnast. When she was 10 years old she went to classes for hours each week and loved it. She was totally devoted. Movement is one of her gifts and strengths; however, she was having difficulty for a long time mastering one skill, a cartwheel.

Her skill level was beyond a regular cartwheel and she was working on an advanced one where she flipped over with no hand support on the mats—an aerial—and she had been working so hard on it. But she couldn't, as they say in gymnastics, "land it."

One thing that gymnastics does very well is to teach strong foundations of each movement so you can build on your next level of difficulty. The athletes focus on strength, flexibility, and skills. My daughter worked and worked but she just could not keep her hands up during that darn move. She was very frustrated as was her coach because she had all the basics needed to master this move, yet week after week I would pick up a frustrated and defeated girl.

Finally, one night I noticed a different beat to her step as she walked to the car. She sort of skipped over to me after this practice. She jumped into the car and said, "I nailed it. I finally landed my aerial!"

I said, "Fantastic! How did you do that?"

She said, "Oh, I finally let go of being afraid I would fall and accepted the fact that could happen. When I let go of the fear, I didn't need my hands anymore."

Letting go is a beautiful thing. It really is about the space that is created when we are able to let go. It leaves room for something else to arrive and take its place. The letting go part feels like the heavy lifting of this step and the space created feels like the reward. It reminds me of the saying by musicians that it is the space between the notes that makes the music sing. The beauty of letting go is in the space between the letting go and the moment when something new arrives to fill the space you created. Hopefully, you will have some choice about what moves in next.

I have wandered around the land of letting go since I was a child. I really did not understand what was going on in my home of origin until I was about 12 years old. About this time, out of desperation, I started visiting the priests at the rectory of my church. I went and mostly just cried. They told me, "Amor Vincit Omnia." Love Conquers All.

Okay, I thought, *I can do that.* I went home, painted it on the walls in my bedroom, and tried to love the pain out of my home. That didn't work because I didn't have the whole formula yet. I needed some of the other missing parts. I got that when I went to Alateen meetings at 16 years old and learned the wisdom that I would carry with me my entire life. That was when I learned that just love is not enough and that letting go was really where it was at. *Now that is something I could learn to do*, I thought. Now, if I can just learn to let go.

The Gargoyle in the Driveway

When my children were really young, I found we all had meltdowns—usually from exhaustion and hunger—somewhere between 4 and 6 pm. A friend called that time the arsenic hour. It was after my work and the kids' daycare and I was trying desperately to get some food into all of us. It was a mess. I noticed that things would often get even worse when my husband walked in the door at the end of his long and exhausting day—just one more tired soul joining the insanity. I realized that this otherwise great father was bringing home all the stress and baggage from his day at the office, and it got to the point that I was really dreading his coming home.

Then I had an idea. At a landscape store, I bought a stone head of a gargoyle with a funny facial expression and put it in the driveway in the rock wall where my husband parked his car. I told him about it and asked him to try an experiment: sit for a few minutes in his car looking at the gargoyle until he could change his mind set and LEAVE all of his issues from the office in the car and not carry them into the house. Since he felt just as frustrated as I, he agreed to try it. The agreement was that he would release all of that stress swirling around in his head into the car before he walked into the house. It was like he had to put his work hat down and pick up his home hat until tomorrow. He could pick it all up again, if he chose, on his way to work.

It worked. Those minutes of quiet for my husband shifted his spirit and his attitude. He let the tension go and walked into the house more centered, a calming force, bringing relief to a tired band of warriors.

Put It Down for a While

We can't always just let something go like my daughter did with her fear of falling. Maybe we can learn to put it down for a while, as my husband did for those many years. You then get more control over what enters and takes your precious time and energy. That gargoyle was still in our driveway 20 years later and my husband used it as a reminder to pause, release, and then enter our home.

I walk the Grace Trail with many cancer survivors at various cancer centers. They are all at different stages of recovery and living with this disease. One of these courageous women shared a technique with me that worked for her in letting go and managing her fears. She described how paralyzed she was with fear after receiving her diagnosis and going through treatment—it was all she could think of. Then she had to go back to work. She decided to try to not think about it for just one hour when she was working. She said that every time that fear came up again and stopped her, she would say to it, "I have saved time for you at 5:00 when I get out of work. I will talk to you then." She would push it out of her mind as she made herself concentrate on what was needing attention. She found that as she practiced this, the amount of time that she was able to divert her attention from her disease lengthened and eventually she could get through most of the day productively. It felt so much better.

But really, how does letting go happen? It is not always enough to tell ourselves to just let a thought or emotion go! If it was enough, it wouldn't be such a struggle.

5 Steps Toward Letting Go

1. Be aware of the feeling—notice it and just feel it, attaching no judgment or criticism.

2. Let it come up, allow the emotion to exist without you taking any action.

3. Stay with it; focus on the feeling and not your thoughts, which will try and distract you. Get to know it well without diverting your attention because it may be uncomfortable, painful, or scary.

4. Let it run its course. Give it permission to work

its way out, sit with it, drop the judgment and the self-criticism, and just feel it.

5. Get allies to help you with this if need be. Therapists, coaches, ministers, teachers and friends are all examples of allies who you may call on for assistance.

Acknowledge the feeling and work through it with curiosity and compassion, hear it, and let it be heard and felt by you. We have to sometimes give these tough emotions attention for them to lessen their impact on us and we let them go.

The Grace Trail can walk you through the process, but it may only take you so far each time. Keep asking those questions and, like layers of an onion, they are removed as you get closer to what lies within.

The relief that follows the release of a feeling or situation is like none other. It is almost like you hear a whooshing sound as you let go and what was behind, rushes forward. I know when I have released something because creativity and spontaneity start to flow.

Letting go can be scary. Here are four ways that may make it more manageable for you.

Four types of release and letting go

1. Put it down forever

Look away from it, focus elsewhere, and do not dwell on the problem or perceived threat. Throw it away, walk away, just stop doing it or participating in it.

2. Put it down for a while

> I sometimes refer to this as utilizing healthy distractions. We can't always put something down and walk away forever, but we hopefully can put it down for a while and turn our attention elsewhere and pick it up again later.

> Create distance so you can choose a different perspective that is true but helps you to move in the direction of your choice.

3. Put little pieces and parts of it down

> Spread out the letting go process. You may not be able to put the whole thing down but is there a piece of it you can release? And then, over time, another?

4. Don't pick it up

> Here it comes again—let it pass by you or through you.

> Allow others pick it up if they wish but don't you touch it.

Once I wander through the process of "what to let go of" and the "how to let go of it" and get to the place of actually letting go, this can unleash energy that is transformational.

Emotions have energy that can get lodged in your body, preventing you from moving forward, feeling free and content.

Letting go can allow your emotions and energy to flow by unblocking them.

You can't make what has happened not have happened. What you can do is get more comfortable being uncomfortable while it hopefully works its way out of you. After that jolt of emotion from an experience is lessened, you have the space to observe it instead of reacting—and then you can hopefully choose your response.

Fear of Failure: Advice from a Lawyer

When I finished my first book, I went to a copyright lawyer.

As I stood up to leave after our meeting, he asked, "Can you stand to hear the word 'no'?"

That question stopped me. I hate the word no, and I was not expecting many no's. I thought if I wrote this book and published it the world would rush forward to buy it. What was he talking about?

He went on to say, "The best ideas and the greatest inventions are sitting in bureau drawers, attics, or boxes in the cellar. People hear a few no's and they give up, dejected and discouraged, and go home. If you are going any further, then get used to 'no.' You will have to learn to depersonalize rejection, hear that 'no,' and move on. If you can't do that, then stop now."

Those wise words helped me to wrestle with my fear of failure. I have not conquered that fear but I have learned to manage it. Here's a strategy a friend shared with me when life hits me on the side of the head with a disappointment or rejection. I call that an **AFGO**, which stands for *Another Freakin' Growth Opportunity.*

Start asking these questions as you release your fear of failure; reframe it with a perspective that gets the desired result.
Ask yourself:

- What lesson is here for me to learn?

- How is this an opportunity for growth?

- What can I take forward with me to my next challenge and do it better?

Framing challenges as learning opportunities will keep those great ideas, books, and products out of the closet and put them in the hands of those who need them! As I am able to take the emotion out of hearing rejection, I am able to look for other perspectives that help me to stay in the game.

And, at times, the closer I get to what I need to release, the more I want to squirm away from it. I notice people turn from the uncomfortable and painful, myself included, thinking we are letting go when we really are not. We can fool ourselves into believing we did indeed let go when maybe we really didn't.

Four "fake" types of letting go

1. Bury it emotionally. This is when we ignore our body and mind connection and do not acknowledge when it is trying to let us know something needs attention. We thought we let it go but we just stuffed it inside of us.

2. Blame others or become a victim. (There are truly victims in the world and I am not referring to them here; instead, we are referring to when you are not actually the victim but merely feel like it.)

   a. Refuse to take responsibility for your part in it.

   b. Look outside of self for why, who, and what is responsible.

3. Distract or anesthetize self.

   a. Engage in activities to distract yourself from feeling the emotions or taking action needed (shopping, eating, gambling, internet, etc.).

   b. Engage in unhealthy choices that lessen your pain and discomfort, numb your senses, distract you, and keep you stuck (medications, substances, alcohol, etc.).

4. Denial and dump it

   a. Let go when you really should hold on.

   b. Let go when action is called for,

The Language of Release and Letting Go

Release . . . Relief . . . Revitalize . . . Reclaim . . . Renew

"It is okay if it happens and it is okay if it doesn't. I am going to still give it my all." That is the language of truly letting go. Our intentions and our efforts are really all that we can control. We can hope, pray, dream, visualize, and work hard but we must surrender to the fact that outcome is usually not in our control.

Listen to yourself when you talk about releasing something.

Are you saying?

> I **won't** let go of . . .
> OR
> I **can't** let go of . . .

I won't is when you are making a choice. I can't is when you are recognizing the reality and limitations of the situation. It can be really hard to tell the difference between *won't* and *can't* but it is essential.

One way that helps me to be clear on what I am telling myself is to say it out loud to someone else. This has two purposes. The first is to let that person hear you and tell you what they think you said. Be clear in what you are asking of them. You may not want feedback; you just need them to listen and tell you what they heard you say. The other reason to say it aloud is for you to hear yourself. I find it hard to fool myself and continue telling a story when I am being witnessed by someone else.

Trust the person whom you select to have this conversation with because generally people are inclined to tell you what to do. You may not want or need that. Most friends' and relatives' advice is usually the advice they need to give themselves. Remember, you are the one who must live with the consequences of letting go, not them.

If you only remember one thing from this chapter, let it be this:

The next time you are in a challenge or struggle, make sure you ask and answer these two questions as soon as possible:

What is in my control?
AND then
What is out of my control?

Then focus on what is in your control as quickly as possible. This will help you to protect your precious energy, stop fighting battles you cannot win and focus on what's important. This is how you become more resilient.

Hard things happen in our lives—heavy issues. Sometimes it is not about what happens but it is about how we hold onto those things and how long we hold onto them that makes the difference.

Letting go takes a belief in yourself that you are worth it.

Loving and letting go. I thought I had it all figured out and then I ran straight into the challenge of acceptance—more of that in the next chapter.

Switchbacks

Choose one of these and do it whenever you are inclined to let something go. Then stand back and watch the response and changes in you.

- Put on a music video and dance to it. Enjoy the energy of release as you work it off through movement.

- Go to the water's edge of a lake, harbor, river, or ocean and stand at a spot where you can safely throw rocks into the water. Think of what you want to let go of as you throw the rocks into the water.

- Pick up something heavy like an old dictionary and carry it with you for a while. Feel the strain of carrying something not necessary for an extended period. Then put it down and feel the relief of letting go.

- Write down what you want to or need to let go of. Put it in a container and put it in the freezer. Leave it there. Take it out and read it in a week. Experience the energy of putting it down for a while.

- Find a private place and moment. Start to walk gently and breathe gently. As you walk, with each slow footfall say, "Let [step] go [step]" as you shake your hands with the rhythm of your step. Feel what it is like to shake off some energy of release.

- In a private moment, look in the mirror and explain to yourself why you continue to hold on when you really want to let go. If you don't believe yourself, then call in an ally to help.

- Punch a pillow and feel the energy of release.

- Go to the top of a mountain, a deserted beach, or big field and yell… someplace where it is safe and okay to make noise. You don't have to scream and irritate your throat. This can be just a good healthy yell. Elongate the noise and feel the relief. Picture it coming out of your body as you release this sound and energy to the world.

Questions to take with you on the Trail

1. What is in my control? What is out of my control?

> And then focus all your energies on what is in your control.

2. _____ and _____ and _____ really scare me.

> What is the probability that each of those may actually happen?
> What do I need to let go of?

3. What is changing? What am I resisting?

> What is it I need to let go of?
> How can I do that?

4. Where in my life have I felt like a victim?

> How can I release that?

> How can I take responsibility for my part? Who can help me?

5. I have the right to change my mind.

> Where do I want to do this? Where do I need to do this?

Chapter 6

What do I need to
accept in my life?

*And, if I can't accept it,
can I at least acknowledge it?*

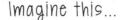

Imagine this...

It is a cold, crisp, winter day just after a storm. The snow is piled high in drifts. The silence and quiet is peaceful as everyone is inside, snuggled and warm. I pause, looking around. There's plenty of time to take it all in. It is just right for observation and reflection.

When I sit quietly and listen, what do I hear inside of me that needs acceptance?

At this point on the Grace Trail in Plymouth, you would be in the middle of a large field. If it were June and the grass had not yet been mowed and baled for hay, you would be fortunate enough to be on a path surrounded by four feet of swaying, beautiful grass and wild flowers. Birds would be nesting in the grass and bunny sightings are abundant. I call it the field of loving awareness. I always encourage those who I am walking with to be quiet and just listen in this field and to listen to this field.

The Essence of Acceptance

- Acceptance requires that you observe and notice what is going on—not only *around* you but also *within* you.

- "I consider the possibility that everything is happening as it is meant to happen" is true acceptance.

- Once you accept, serenity and peace are possible.

- To accept what you can't control allows you to stop fighting battles you cannot win.

- Acceptance breeds choice and it is not the same as giving up or feeling victimized.

- Acceptance follows acknowledgment.

- To acknowledge is the ability to see it and hear it clearly.

- Compassion, courage, and honesty are often necessary for acceptance.

- Sometimes the hardest things to accept are those things about ourselves.

Shhh! This is the quiet step of Grace.

Deep down inside us there is wisdom, a deep knowing that lies within our hearts and souls. For us to hear that voice, we have to be quiet and allow it to speak, and that is why I call this the quiet step on the Grace Trail. In the stillness, we can bring our curiosity and questions to a place where the answers are waiting for us to find them.

This step of Grace sits between the two questions of Release and Challenge that set it up nicely to encourage you to check in with yourself.

It follows Release, where we let go and push things out of the way that are blocking our vision. Letting go can be a hard thing to do but this difficulty in letting go is exactly how our pile of what needs acceptance grows taller. We tend to ignore the tough issues and put them off for another day. It is often what is out of our control that demands our acknowledgment. If we find the courage and stamina to look at what needs acceptance more often, it gets easier and the pile gets smaller.

Acceptance precedes Challenge on the Grace Trail. We access awareness and introspection before we commit to action. That is how we can make sure our precious energy is going where it needs to go.

Acceptance lives on a spectrum, with one end being acceptance and the other, acknowledgement. There are different degrees of both as we move between the two, sometimes inching along toward acceptance only to be pulled back again to the beginning. It can take years for both acknowledgment and acceptance to happen, if ever. Many people live in total denial, with situations in their lives never acknowledged or accepted.

Acceptance will take place only when there is a willingness to look at your inner life and feelings. It is easy to be distracted and so appealing to look the other way. Staying aware in life and being present for as much as possible is necessary to live your life fully. Our brain tugs us back into our subconscious; the world calls to us and we don't even realize when we go on automatic pilot. Because of this we often miss precious opportunities that sit right in front of us.

Life is a generous, patient teacher. It gives you the opportunity to learn your lessons over and over and over again until you get it.

The Parakeet

One early spring morning, I was working in my home office when there was a knock at the door. My friend from next door said, "There's a parakeet in your driveway."

"What?" I live in the Northeast and we don't have parakeets living around here, at least not on this side of bars, or so I thought.

"Are you sure it's not a goldfinch?" I asked.

Her reply was, "It is yellow and green and blue. I'm sure it's a parakeet."

Curious, I walked to the end of my driveway and there indeed stood a little yellow, blue, and green parakeet. It was obvious that this bird was used to humans because we could get close and he just kept pecking at the ground, looking for food. With very little discussion, we parents and animal lovers immediately decided that we had to catch the little bird. We were certain that he just could not wait to get back home, safe and sound and didn't consider any other option. We thought of the hawks, so numerous in this area, and swung into action without discussion. We had visions of some child quite upset because someone left the cage open and his beloved friend escaped.

When we got really close to the bird, he panicked and struggled and flew up to a tree. He was kind of awkward, as if flying any distance was not natural to him. Now what? How do we save this bird? After a quick phone call to my vet, who gave me a few tips, I decided to go out later and, if the bird was still there, to try again.

I went back to work and a while later as I walked to the end of my driveway to get the mail, there sat the bird looking at me nonchalantly, scratching for food. This time I was equipped with a cage that my neighbor had dropped off. I positioned the cage with an open door, and my first strategy, as the vet suggested, was to hold my finger out, hoping the bird would just hop on—no luck.

Second option, I threw down some seed in a path that led right up to my cage, hoping he would jump in quite relieved to be "home" again—no luck.

I chatted with the bird quietly, sidled up closer, and tried to grab it. As it flew away again, I reasoned, I had given my all to be the great pet rescuer. I felt that I had done as much as I could and sort of forgot about the bird, who looked down at me from the telephone wire, again.

The next day, as I was walking my dog about a half mile from home, from out of nowhere, the parakeet startled me by flying directly at my face and then landing on the sidewalk in front of me. Well, this is a new challenge. What is it with this bird? What does he want from me? Now, I have nothing to catch him with so I have to surrender my thoughts to the dangers that this little guy was facing. I was feeling quite protective and frustrated as I couldn't help him or her out once again. As I started to walk away from the situation, another neighbor saw me staring up at the telephone line where the parakeet was now sitting. He inquired about what was happening and I explained and showed him the bird. As he walked away, he said he was going home to get a net, ladder, and his two little boys because they were going to catch that bird. I thought, *Good luck*, as we walked away.

That night, a fierce storm, Hurricane Irene, blew in. During the many hours stuck inside, listening to that howling wind and watching those trees bend almost to breaking, I must admit that I mentioned that little bird a couple of times to my husband. "That poor little parakeet is never going to make it through this!"

The day after the storm, I was walking my dog on a totally different route and, lo and behold, that amazing parakeet was sitting on the sidewalk right in front of us! This time, we just said hello and walked by. I had finally surrendered.

On the way home we encountered a woman standing on the sidewalk staring up into the tree. I looked at her and said, "You looking at the parakeet?"

"Yes," she said and then she added, "I am going to go get a net."

"Good luck with that," I replied.

It was at this moment that I discovered I had a new attitude about this little guy. He didn't need my help at all. *He made it through a hurricane.* I started considering that these may be the best days of his life—cage-free, independent, and so resourceful, maybe he was really enjoying himself. I finally heard the message from this resilient, tiny soul. I was reminded to look outside my perspective and reconsider my assumption that had unconsciously moved me to act—to try catching a bird whose destiny did not include a cage.

What is Acceptance?

- Acceptance is a decision to experience a situation or process without trying to change it, leave, or argue and protest.

- To accept what you cannot control allows you to stop fighting battles you cannot win.

- Acceptance breeds choice and is not the same as giving up or becoming a victim.

- Acceptance may include action.

Acceptance sounds like:

"I consider the possibility that everything is happening as it is meant to happen."

That doesn't mean you have to like it, agree with it, or that you cannot take action to change it.

Buried within all of us is everything we don't like about ourselves, I have found over the decade of coaching that loving acceptance of ourselves seems to be a big challenge for many people, myself included. We seemed to have learned an aversion to self-acceptance—the internal critic is louder than the positive self-perception.

We also seem to bury what we don't like about others and situations. Our natural inclination is to avoid, look away, or pretend it is not there, which is easy and quick in the short run but does not work for the long run. Our need to look away starts to have increased importance in our life. Those emotions and situations start screaming for our attention to be noticed. By acknowledging and accepting them, they get quiet, and once quiet, they no longer rule us.

If you can't accept something, first work on simply acknowledging it.

What is Acknowledgment?

- To acknowledge is to see it and hear it clearly and truthfully, even if you don't like it.

- To be acknowledged is to be seen and heard clearly.

- Acknowledgment precedes acceptance.

- Acknowledgment sounds like this: "It is what it is," or "I hear you."

Everyone has a need to be truly seen and heard. We yearn for deep connection with others by simply being acknowledged. Some things are never acknowledged, therefore they can never be accepted. That is called denial.

Acknowledgment always precedes acceptance. Once something is acknowledged then acceptance is a possibility but not a guarantee.

Sometimes we have acknowledgment but never move into acceptance.

We can have both acknowledgment and acceptance though they may be years apart.

Acknowledgment and acceptance help us to surrender and therein lies freedom and harmony.

To acknowledge the parts of our lives that are difficult and messy as well as those that are good, means we are acknowledging the full spectrum—the good, the bad, and the ugly. Welcome to adulthood.

The Kayak

I got back in my kayak again last summer. I couldn't resist the allure of kayaking with a group of friends. I had planned to sell the kayak following a great white shark attack off a beach in my town last summer.

I had the winter to mull over the prospects for selling or not. There was plenty of discussion around this area about sharks and I was pretty sure I would never float again in that boat. Every time I walked by that newly posted sign they placed on the beach that reads:

Potential hazards in these waters may include:

Rip current
Heavy surf
Dangerous marine life to include:
sharks, seals, jelly fish etc.

USE AREA AT OWN RISK

I thought, *Well that was pretty clear.* There probably are sharks in these waters and they may swim under my boat, or worse.

We never had great whites around here before, but apparently there's a colony of large seals that no longer migrate out of here to colder waters in the summer. They now stay in this area all year long as it is rich in food, and the sharks follow the seals because seal is their favorite food.

Granted, the young women who were attacked last year knowingly steered their kayaks toward a recent shark attack on a seal. So they did go into waters where sharks were known to be feeding. But sharks swim, and they swim all over the place looking for food.

Last spring when I was in California, we were at a beach that great whites were known to frequent, again, for the seal population. That didn't seem to stop people from surfing, paddle boarding, and swimming and they all seemed to make it to shore safely that day.

So, I had become aware of the danger and I had acknowledged it. I made the conscious choice to get back in the boat, accepting the fact that there may be dangerous marine life below me. Sounds like life, doesn't it?

My thoughts were, as long as I minimized the possibility of an encounter with a shark, the possibility of joy and fun outweighed the risk for me. As I had acknowledged the possibilities, I chose to take a kayak trip with a group one evening last summer. There really is nothing like an adventure with some friends paddling along a beautiful shore, enjoying the sun shining on the water, and the warm breeze.

Once we started, we stayed close to the shore and went into the harbor not the open ocean. At one point, my husband yelled over to me, "Hey, you are so close to shore, why don't you just get out and walk to town?" He was right—my paddle was actually hitting the bottom! I did eventually venture out deeper into the harbor and it was a wonderful experience that I hope to repeat, keeping in mind that there are no guarantees. I had decided to curtail where and when I would kayak to minimize my chance of an unwanted encounter, but it was not going to stop me.

The Language of Acceptance

Aware . . . Awake . . . Acknowledge . . . Accept . . . Alive

Acceptance: "I consider the possibility that everything is happening as it is meant to happen."

I can learn to accept my feelings or a difficult situation and be free from them.

I am okay.

You are okay.

It is okay. (You may not like it and you can still take action.)

I can begin to accept slowly, maybe just a bit at a time.

I am worthy and lovable just as I am.

I am willing and I am able.

I encourage you to step up and nurture your courage; be willing to look at and be with difficult emotions and feelings. Get help from professionals if you need it. This may include therapists, counselors, ministers, support groups, and coaches.

The Language of Acknowledgment:
"It is what it is." Or "I hear you."

I can try to look at my feelings.

I can feel my feelings.

I can handle them or get some help in handling them.

There are situations in my life that I do not like, make me uncomfortable or are painful. I am going to take the courageous step and just acknowledge those situations. Position it like the thoughts listed above it.

Shhhhhh! Let's Get Quiet

Acceptance is the quiet step of Grace. This is the time when we are quiet, observe and listen within ourselves with no action taken or envisioned..

Here is one way to calm your brain to access your wisdom, one very simple way you can quiet your mind anywhere.

Follow the sensation of one of your breaths—the expansion and contraction of your chest, the feeling of each inhale compared to the warmth of each exhale, the sound and feeling of your breathing from the inside of you.

Now follow the feeling of five more breaths as they enter and exit your body.

Imagine these breaths around your heart filling it with gentle love—no criticism or judgment, just love.

When you hear your thoughts starting again, focus back on the internal sensation of your breath and connect with the good feelings that you hold.

There are many other resources available for you to learn to quiet your mind. My favorites are meditation and walking, and I encourage you to explore different ways that may work for you.

Becoming More Aware and Moving Closer to Acceptance

There is research that indicates that observing your feelings rather than your thoughts increases your awareness more quickly.

When faced with your next choice and experiencing some confusion, ask and answer:

- What does my head think?

- What does my heart feel?

- What does my soul know to be true?

Serenity is when your head, heart, and soul are all on the same page.

When you pause in your life, get quiet, and notice the entire picture, then you can make choices about different perspectives and ways of thinking. The quiet is the time when the mind is still enough to hear the answers that are there for you. There is a place in awareness where you can stand beside your experience and witness it without the emotional response to it. From that point, we are able to make conscious decisions instead of being dragged by our past, our fears, and our emotions.

So, with the right question and a quiet mind, you are able to find the answer that lies within. You will receive the answer that is yours alone, the answer that is waiting to be found.

Five Steps Toward Acceptance

1. Observe the feeling with no intention of doing anything about it.

2. Think about your relationship to that feeling.

3. Let it be there with no judgment or criticism.

4. Patiently let it be what it is until the energy of that emotion runs out.

5. See if this helps your relationship with this emotion, to change, or if the emotional charge lessens or disappears.

The Danger of Managing
Our Thoughts and Emotions

One of our challenges in life is to better manage our thoughts and emotions so we can move in the direction of our choice. Acknowledgment and acceptance can remove the electrical charge from an emotion so we can better be with it and manage our emotions. This helps us to think and respond instead of quickly and emotionally react. It is only then that we can make more of the conscious decisions we need to live the life we want to live.

However, there is a downside to effectively managing your thoughts and emotions. Sometimes you do not need to, and should not, manage them. Instead just be with the experience and the emotion that arises. Sometimes we have to let the human experience guide us no matter how we feel about that. There is a lot to learn there also.

There are other times that I am unable to manage my emotions as they may overwhelm me or I allow someone else's emotions to disregulate mine. This frequently happens when I am not on top of my game, so the following is what I do when feeling that way.

I learned this in Al-Anon many years ago and it is called:

HALT!

Stop and ask these questions:

Am I . . .

Hungry?

Angry?

Lonely?

Tired?

This process often helps me to pinpoint the cause of my feeling out of balance and how to hopefully to remedy it. It is not always a deep, soul-searching solution that is needed. Sometimes it is quite simple.

I have had experiences where I wanted something so much that I ignored signs and signals from my body that were screaming for me to pay attention. I plowed through them and stomped over them only to find that I should have listened.

When I willfully ignore the signs, it's usually when my expectations are unrealistic and I'm hoping for an outcome that is just not possible. It's really hard to figure out because, although hope can move mountains and although we want to move those mountains, we have to be sure they are the right mountains.

Willie Wisdom

We were out one evening walking the dog. It was very dark and we were approaching the end of a street that ran beside the woods ahead of us when my dog, Willie, stopped short. Now this was not your usual tug on the leash stop. This was a full four-footed, brakes-on stop, bracing his legs, and refusing to budge. Willie weighs only 6 pounds so it is not really a challenge to move him. He also thinks he knows what is best and frequently tries to change direction and lead us. Sometimes we let him and sometimes we don't.

My husband looked at me and said, "I am so sick of this dog telling us what to do. Willie, come on!" as he tugged and began to drag the dog forward. Willie's brakes were not releasing. My husband, frustrated, picked him up and we began to go forward.

That was when we heard them: a howling, barking pack of coyotes right in the woods, unseen, just feet away from us. They were sitting in wait for us with this delicious little morsel of potential food in our arms. We froze as the hair went up on my neck and arms. Terror! We looked at each other, turned, and started to walk really fast back toward home in the direction Willie had been telling us we needed to go.

Now, this doesn't mean that we listen to Willie all the time. But I will tell you this, I take notice when I receive 6 pounds of resistance, all four brakes are on, and Willie just won't budge.

Knowing when to manage our thoughts and emotions takes wisdom. It may look like this: take a few steps that way and then listen, wag your tail, decide on the next step and take a few steps in the other direction, listen, and decide—keep doing that and eventually you will find your way.

When we learn to step into the place of quiet we then tap into and access the power of quiet. That is when insight happens. Have you noticed when you get your best and most creative ideas? They arrive in the shower, walking, exercising, driving alone—get the picture? It happens in the quiet and quiet is probably not going to happen often unless you make it happen.

Awareness, acknowledgment, and acceptance thrive in the

quiet. Please join them there as often as possible because se-renity hangs out with them there.

To live your life fully, you need to encourage yourself to look behind the appearance of things on the surface and then go deeper. We usually see what we want to see and not what is actually in front of us. We look but we may not truly com-prehend. A good question helps, especially when paired with a receptive and open heart—that is the best opportunity we have to gain wisdom.

Acceptance nurtures harmony with yourself and the world and joy can appear when you feel in tune and relaxed.

I still strive for acceptance in my life. Things just constantly change and there seems to always be more waiting for me in that pile. Yup. Working on it.

Switchbacks

Choose one of these and do it whenever you feel there is something calling for your attention within and you are hav-ing a hard time seeing it and hearing it. Then stand back, no-tice, and observe the response.

- Be quiet. Turn off the computer, phone, fax, text, Facebook, LinkedIn, TV and every other way the world has to reach you, distract you, and drain you. Do this for 10 minutes every day. Silence. Just sit and stare. Access the power of quiet.

- Acknowledge yourself. Identify one thing you did

right today. Maybe it is something big that you would like to congratulate yourself for. Say what needs to be said and what you are yearning to hear. You deserve it. Access the nutrients that feed your desire to do better.

- Take a warm bath. Sink low into the water, and then feel the silence. Just be quiet and listen. Immerse yourself in the sensory experience.

- Exercise vigorously or dance to music and at the end, just be quiet and notice what may be calling for your attention within. Wake up your senses and turn off your thinking and then listen.

- Meditate. The best kind of meditation is the kind that you will actually do. Try different types of meditation and see what works for you. You can get programs online, at meditation classes, watch videos on You-Tube, or read about it in a book.

- For me, there is nothing like a walking meditation. Just put your walking shoes on and go with no intention other than to quietly move forward. See what happens when you pair quiet with relaxing, repetitive movement. It may be yoga, swimming, knitting, painting or whatever… Notice and just listen.

Questions to take with you on the Trail

1. If I were able to stop fighting it, avoiding it, or denying it then what could I acknowledge? What could I accept?

2. I sit quietly and still my thoughts as I continually drift back to calm. As I breathe in the quiet, I will ask, "What is sitting right in front of me, calling out to be heard?"

3. When faced with your next choice and experiencing some confusion, ask and answer:

   • What does my head think?

   • What does my heart feel?

   • What does my soul know to be true?

Serenity is when your head, heart, and soul all have the same answer.

4. What am I ready to ask for?

   What am I willing to accept?

5. Today's official Worry List includes these three things: _____, _____, and _____.

   • What things can I actually change or influence?

   • What do I need to acknowledge?

   • What do I need to accept?

Chapter 7

Even though my plate is full,
what is my challenge?

Imagine this...

The days are getting longer, lighter, and warmer as spring arrives. The sun is waking up the earth and all of its inhabitants. The vibrant energy of inspiration, enthusiasm, and new life is everywhere. The once dormant land and gardens are now alive with green sprouts poking through the moist soil, and buds bursting open on the trees.

What do I want to plant in my life?

At this point on the Grace Trail in Plymouth, you would see the harbor ahead of you as you briskly walked down a gentle hill on a quiet road between two beautiful fields. When I walked with the Girl Scouts and the yoga camp for teens, they skipped and laughed down this part of the Trail. That is the get up and go energy of Challenge. I have not been able to get any of the adults to skip down that road with me . . . yet.

The Essence of Challenge

- Challenge includes action and change.

- Inspiration and creativity, as well as necessity and desperation, can be the sparks that ignite and spur you into action.

- Honesty, courage, and curiosity live within challenge.

- If your challenge has meaning and purpose for you, it will feed your drive, sustain it and make it more likely to happen.

- Challenging yourself by making conscious choices will move you closer to where you want and need to be.

- Challenge does not have to be a tangible, physical act. Challenge and change can be about attitude and perspective.

- A challenge may be something you give to yourself or someone else.

- Designing your challenge and stating the intention aloud or writing it as a goal will make it more likely to happen.

- Although they are all part of a challenge, the energy of change and action are different from the energy of visualizing, planning, and goal setting.

- Visually imagining what you wish to create and choosing your next steps from there will carry you closer to that vision.

- Self-judgment, criticism, fear of failure, and humiliation crush creativity.

- Change is hard. Most change occurs with struggle, turmoil, and uncertainty as part of the picture.

When I was younger I thought I had all the time and energy in the world. I committed without much thought and never realized how precious each moment was. Now I realize if I am saying "yes" to one thing then I am saying "no" to something else.

Here is a challenge for you:

Between the time you put your feet on the floor in the morning and slip them back between the sheets at night, make sure your efforts point toward what matters most to you, as much as humanly possible.

Wake yourself up throughout the day and ask yourself, "What

is my challenge, right now?" If you are not pointed in the right direction… recalculate your route.

I call it, "Living life awake."

Grace Trail helps you to do this. The questions lead you to reflect before you commit and get into action. They help you bring a fresh perspective to the routine of your day. You match your energy and intention to the moment and that helps to ensure you are working on what matters most.

There is something really special about commitment. It should not be done lightly because it takes a certain combination of focus, direction, and determination to see something through. I am determined to not make commitments I can't complete.

That is the sweet spot of the challenge that I just gave to you. It is up to you to be aware of those moments where you have a choice for how you use your resources. Time, energy, focus, money, enthusiasm, and creativity are finite resources and must be dealt out with careful thought.

Bridge Jumper

Every summer my family vacationed on Martha's Vineyard, an island off the coast of Massachusetts. We biked, picnicked, and, except for me, jumped off a bridge into the ocean—for fun.

I was always the self-designated photographer of this annual rite of summer, until one summer I made the decision to break ranks from the other mothers and photographers on the jetty and *become a bridge jumper.* I felt like it was my rite of passage as a vacationer on this fabulous island.

Let me set the scene for you. This was not just any bridge—this was the bridge that was featured in the movie *Jaws*.

For those who haven't seen it, *Jaws* is a movie about a killer white shark that attacks vacationing swimmers on "Amity Island." It was filmed on Martha's Vineyard and one of the most memorable scenes was filmed at this very bridge. While the people on the beach are scanning the ocean to reassure themselves that the danger has passed, the giant shark is gliding silently under *this* bridge into the pond on the other side where small children are swimming.

That is the bridge I was going to jump from. Could I have chosen a spot with any more drama? Having a 10-foot freefall into the chilling Atlantic Ocean is plenty but now I had the image of that shark to deal with.

Well, I had decided, no matter what, time was running out and we would be going home soon, ***so this was the day***.

I walked onto the bridge with my daughter and her friend, both veteran jumpers, and left my husband on the beach with the camera for the big moment. As I walked closer to the place where I would jump, I started to hear all the previous excuses that kept me from jumping other years. What if I hit a jelly fish? Maybe the tide is not quite high enough? Maybe I should wait for the clouds to go away so I can see shadows better under the water.

My heart was literally pounding in my chest, I was breathing so fast for what seemed like my last breath as I climbed over the railing to stand on the edge and scan the water below for any sign of fins slicing through the current.

I heard from my veteran bridge-jumping daughter, "OK, Mom, let's jump on the count of three. OK?" She reached out and held my hand, yelling "One-two-three!!!"

At the last second, I pulled my hand back and my daughter jumped in alone as I clutched the bridge with a white-knuckle grip. I must admit that I felt a bit of shame allowing her to go into those shark-infested waters without me—but not enough to get me off the railing. As I stood there and watched her splash into the ocean, all my maternal instincts totally disintegrated, and my first thought was, "How do I get off this bridge without getting wet?"

The entire crowd on the bridge was looking at me and yelling, cheering me on. They saw my cowardly heart and I heard, "Go for it!" "You can do it!" "Jump!" and from the water, "Mom, come on!"

I am really not sure where the courage came from but I took a breath and I jumped. The time between leaving that edge and hitting the water seemed like an eternity, surrounded by air and wind and sun and fear!

And then SPLASH! into the cool, blue water. Bubbles and silence engulfed me as I shot below the surface, touched bottom, and then pushed off toward the surface again. In those few seconds all my trepidation turned into elation and when I came up for air I heard cheering beside me, above me, from the beach, and, best of all, inside me.

It was so much fun that I couldn't wait to do it again. During the next hour, my enthusiasm and bravery empowered and inspired three other mothers to join me in the privileged ranks of intrepid bridge jumpers.

I chose to jump off that bridge after three summers of watching my family and friends having fun without me. Three summers noticing hundreds of people jumping and no one getting hurt. Three summers of gathering my courage and making the commitment to myself. One person's challenge is another's joy.

I used to jump off a bridge at a beach when I was a kid and the water didn't look so far down then. Amazing how my fears seemed to grow with age. Now, the "What if...?" seems to scream louder than the "What fun!" I was determined to get back my edge. I needed to reawaken my sense of adventure because it withers and dies if you don't use it.

I came so close to climbing back over the railing to put it on my to-do list for next year's vacation. The public declaration as I stood on the edge, with everyone watching and cheering me on, was one of the reasons I chose to proceed—another was to avoid humiliation. Hearing my daughter encouraging me was awesome. She and everyone on that bridge were my allies and they wanted it for me. They saw that it was possible when I didn't.

And to have remained on the edge after having pulled my hand from daughter's as she jumped gave me the moment to design it on my terms. Instead of being pulled off the bridge,

I matched my intention and my energy to create the push I needed in just that moment to get the job done.

"This Is the Part of the Show Where We *Dare* to Suck!"

Those are the words that I heard from the famous singer Carole King during one of her concerts on *The Living Room Tour*. She explained to the audience that each night one band member is responsible for bringing a piece of a song, melody, lyric, or an idea to the stage. In front of thousands of people they then throw it out to the other band members and together they improvise and make up a song right then.

As Carole said, some nights they wrote great songs and other nights *they really sucked!*

She went on to explain that this broke the repetition and boredom of singing the same songs over and over, night after night. It kept it fun and challenging for all of them and it kept the process alive. They were willing to take the risk of sounding foolish for the possibility of creating something great.

There were the beginnings of some great songs that came from those improvisational sessions and even some of the melodies that "sucked" were used later in other songs.

When I am challenged to take action and I am afraid, I tell myself that if Carole can "dare to suck" then I can, too.

Pizza Dough

I compare making pizza dough to overcoming my self-doubts. First you throw the unformed ball of dough down on the counter then you knead it with your hands, warm it up, and get it ready it for the rolling pin. Next you put pressure on with the rolling pin and start to slowly push the dough out. It gets bigger and bigger and thinner and thinner with every push as the dough totally transforms and stretches in response to the pressure. At last, it is big enough for your pizza pan and you stop, only to observe the dough immediately start to shrink to a smaller size.

That is what it is like to manage my self-doubts. Just when I get far enough out of my comfort zone and excited about my progress, my self-doubts show up screaming and I start to shrink back. Gratefully, I am getting better at listening to them, calming them and moving past them.

I still stumble forward through many challenges, making mistakes and relearning some lessons. My reserve of wisdom is growing as I embrace the fact that to get that wisdom, I will make mistakes and run into obstacles but I will keep trying. As hard as it is, I try to view these challenges as opportunities for learning and growth. I can take that knowledge into my next challenge and adapt it and get stronger.

I know there are no guarantees except when not trying at all—that outcome is guaranteed.

One of my biggest challenges is to know if the voices of doubt are wisdom or valid fears that I need to listen to. I have some formidable voices of doubt. I try to embrace them now instead of fighting them or trying to silence them. I realize they just want to keep me safe and the bigger the challenge, the louder the voices scream. Those voices want me back in my comfort zone, safe. There are times when they are right and I do need to listen to them.

I do not always know the difference between a valid fear or just plain anxiety. In that case I may proceed slowly with that challenge as I constantly reassess and listen. That is the risk part of challenge—moving forward amidst the fears and calls to return to safety when moving ahead holds no guarantees. Sometimes I ask and do an assessment of the risk, *Is this going to be a fatal error?* Are the risks so high that they are not worth taking? If yes, I ponder longer and may invite others whom I trust to join the discussion. This may actually include some professionals—coaches, therapists, lawyers, designers, marketers, or whoever's expertise may help me to decide. If the answer is no and the risk seems worth it to me, then I proceed down that path as I continue to assess if it all feels right along the way.

Getting Into Action
and Sustaining Our Efforts

A good, hot cup of tea has a lot in common with a challenge. When I make my tea in the morning, I have all the ingredients I need: tea leaves, water, and my mug. But I still don't have a cup of tea. I need more. I need the energy that produces the heat to boil the water so the tea leaves can steep and become a cup of tea.

As with a challenge, it is not enough to have just the components of a great idea and a plan. You also need the energy to make the heat that will move you into action and sustain your efforts until completion.

Enthusiasm, energy, creativity, passion, purpose, meaning, pleasure, love—all of these can provide the impetus for action. Of course, fear, desperation, and a big jolt from life can also give us the steam necessary to muster what we need for commitment and change.

I have found that when my challenges and efforts are tied in with what matters most to me, I get the job done. Passion, purpose, and meaning are my 212 degrees of heat and they create my steam, with the right motivations to get me into the flow and help me to persevere.

The Language of Challenge

Challenge . . . Curiosity . . . Create . . . Choice . . . Courage . . . Commitment.

Here is the language of challenge and commitment:

"This is what I need to do_____."

"I am going to_____ by this date ____ and this time ____."

"I commit to_____ and you will know it is done by_____."

This is NOT the language of challenge and commitment...

> "I think I will..."

> "I probably should do..."

> "I think I probably will..."

> "It would be a good idea to..."

> "I think maybe I probably will..."

That is the language of stuck, of still thinking about it. Those are words I commonly hear from new clients who have never been coached before. There is no challenge or commitment stated in those phrases.

GOALS: Goal setting is also the language of challenge. Creating goals makes your success more likely. Goals are commitments in words and words create our future. They communicate a belief that you are capable, and they focus your attention on your target to help you find ways to get there. Goals that are pursued out of personal desire and self-choice make success more likely.

COURAGE: Courage is the language of challenge. The Latin root for courage is heart. Grace Trail speaks the language of the heart.

Courage has an energy of its own and is necessary for change and challenge. Hope is often the nutrient that feeds courage. Here is what courage sounds like:

> "I will..."

"I can..."

"I am going to try..."

"Even though I am scared, ..."

We all want to be courageous.

How do we get braver? Where does courage live inside us? How do we wake it up and call on it when we really need it? Sometimes I need to rally my courage. At those times, I make a Declaration of Courage and call it forward by encouraging myself. Do you see the word courage in encourage? I acknowledge I need to be brave even though I may be scared. Raise your fist in the air and say it out loud, "It is time to be courageous!"

RESILIENCY: Resiliency is the language of challenge.
It requires us to push through hard times to the other side and it sounds like this:

> "I will learn from my mistakes and failures so I will not make the same mistake in my next challenge."

> "I realize the path ahead has many challenges and obstacles and I will figure it out as I go along."

When my son first entered the Army and went to boot camp, the struggles and challenges often seemed insurmountable. That was the point of boot camp. It challenges soldiers to push through their limitations to a get to a stronger place. At a very intense point for everyone in their training, his drill sergeant yelled, *"Embrace the Suck!"*

I call that the language of challenge...

ALLIES: Allies are a part of the language of challenge especially when those challenges get bigger. What if you did not have to take on this challenge alone? Many times we trudge forward under tremendous strain of a challenge and don't ask for help. Often, we do not need to do this alone or be in isolation.

There are so many points along the challenge route that allies may prove to be an asset and great part of your team. Be creative on how you can possibly include others to both lighten your load and help with the design and decision making during your next challenge.

All the stories in this section are about challenges that were chosen by us. Life is not always that gentle in dealing out its challenges. Many times they are handed over with nonnegotiable terms. Get it done. Do it. Pay the bills. Get to work. Take care of your health. We all have plenty of those challenges.

Sometimes I feel that the better I get at handling my challenges, the faster they seem to come my way.

The more you bring your consciousness to your commitments, the better you become at making your actions more purposeful. That is the challenge in this step. Aim your efforts in the direction of your choosing even if it is one tiny step at a time.

Let's face it, we waste so much of our precious time and energy doing things that may not really matter or that aren't the most important at that moment. Our brain loves to pull us back into the unconscious business and busyness of the day and we all have things that have to get done. Before we know it, the day is gone and we are tired. Stack those days up, they turn into weeks and years, and all of a sudden, we hear ourselves saying, "How did I get here?" "Where did the time go?" We can change that. Okay, now let's get walking on Grace Trail.

Switchbacks

Here are suggestions to access the energy that is in our body. Choose one of these to address your next challenge or rejuvenate your energy when choosing a challenge.

- March. Stand up and march. Put on a marching face and swing your arms. Access the energy of action and determination.

- Shadow box. Bend your knees, shift your weight from foot to foot, punching and jabbing at the air first to your right and then to your left, making sure you cross over your mid-body line to the other side. Punch high, punch low, punch left, punch right, multiple jabs here... single jabs there. Access bursts of strong energy.

- Change how you do one of your everyday tasks. Such as, brush your teeth with your other hand or write with your other hand. Wake up both sides of your brain and make some news connections.

- Drive a different route to a destination when you

have no pressure to arrive at a specific time. Or be the passenger instead of the driver. See what you see on that route that may inform you of your next challenge. Access the energy of calm curiosity.

- Do something outrageous—something that scares you and will bring you closer to your hopes and dreams. Get out of your comfort zone, access the energy of courage. (I am not encouraging recklessness or dangerous choices.) There is a lot to be learned on an adventure.

- Go for a curiosity walk in a book store. Just wander. See what titles and book covers grab your attention and spark your interest. Access the energy of curiosity.

- Buy a jump rope and use it. Let your whole body know that you have every intention of moving forward. Access the energy of enthusiasm and vitality.

- Get out some crayons or markers and some really big sheets of paper and start to doodle. Access the energy of exploring with no negative outcome at all.

- Distract yourself by doing something repetitive like knitting, biking, dancing, drawing, walking. Lose yourself in the moment. Give your brain and your body a break and then access the energy of rejuvenation. Bring it to your next challenge.

- Go skip, swing your arms wide, and smile. It is fun to skip. Access the active energy of joy and see how that feeds your energy for challenges.

Questions to take with you on the Trail

1. What is my WHY for taking on this challenge? Why is it important?

    What is the reason that I need to give my resources to this?

2. Is there a challenge I would like to give someone else in my life?

    How can I deliver it for the impact that I desire?

3. I am looking at my biggest challenge.

    How persistent am I in pursuing it?

    What is distracting me?

    What can help me to stay focused on what is important?

4. We all need allies to sustain our momentum.

    How can I create or strengthen my support system?

5. Here is my Challenge: _____

    In order to do this_____

    What do I need to say Yes to?

    What do I need to say No to?

    How do I muster the courage needed?

Chapter 8

Even though nothing is certain...

What can I embrace as possible?

Imagine this...

It is a sunny, warm summer day. I have been yearning for and dreaming about this for a long time. The days are long, relaxed, and luxurious as the flowers are bursting with blooms, the bees are buzzing, and the birds are singing. In summer, I feel a part of the ease and flow of the abundance of all that has yet to be harvested.

Where am I ready to bloom and grow in my life?

At this point on the Grace Trail in Plymouth, we have walked the other four questions and we find ourselves on familiar territory with a new twist. We've walked here before, we are closing the loop on the trail, and this time the beautiful surroundings will help to feed your imagination to envision both what you desire and what you believe is possible in your life.

The Essence of Embrace

- After walking the first four steps of the Grace Trail process, we arrive at Embrace where we encourage a new direction, feeling, perspective, or attitude to emerge.

- This step can feel like a painter feels when looking at a blank canvas, a gardener feeling rich soil, a dancer hearing great music or a writer faced with a blank page.

- This is when we get to create a more expansive perspective by asking both what we wish for and what we will allow.

- Embracing the mindset that more is indeed possible opens us up to see and receive all that is possible.

- Asking yourself, "What do I want my energy to flow toward?" can consciously change the flow of our energy toward what we desire.

- The energy of embrace is about the big picture and the universe of potential and possibility.

- Having a desirable image of what our future can possibly be increases our focus in that direction and helps sustain our attention for what we hope to create.

- Using images and metaphors of the future we wish to create instructs our brain to search for relevant information to help us on that path.

- This step invites you to think of more spacious, hopeful conditions instead of the evidence that you have collected right in front of you.

- There is an energy and attitude of expansiveness that speaks from hope and asks, "Where to from here?"

Boots On the Trail

The summer when the story of the Grace Trail was brewing in my imagination but still only a rough draft on paper, I was overcome with severe self-doubts. I was afraid no one would care about this. After all, who was I to write a story? Who was I to create a trail? I was entertaining the prospect of just quitting.

On this day, I was walking the trail, soon to become officially the Grace Trail, with two friends, feeling a little melancholy but keeping my doubts to myself.

As we approached the part of the trail leading down to the beach, I noticed something in the grass. When I stopped to investigate, I was startled to see a pair of worn-out boots, un-laced and discarded at the side of the trail. I looked around to see if the owner was nearby, but my friend said that the boots had been there yesterday. All I could think was, "Who do they belong to?" "What are they doing there?"

I was stunned because I was writing the short story, "Walking Off Your War," in which the survivor, who is walking the Grace Trail, kicks her boots off and leaves them on the trail leading down to the beach. This felt eerily like more than a coincidence. It was just like the spot in the story, a message for me from the universe, someone trying to tell me to keep going on this Grace Trail. I decided at that moment to put my own metaphorical boots back on and continue on my Grace Trail adventure, my self-doubts dissipated. I was grateful to have people with me to witness this, though of course, I did photograph those boots left as a sign to me.

I hold the image of those boots on the trail close to my heart as I invite the universe to participate in my hopes and dreams in any way that it chooses. My brain then goes to work scanning the horizon for pathways to get me to my goal. I hope I am aware enough for the arrival of those possibilities because I don't want to miss any of them. I can't afford to miss any of them.

This is the step where it feels like magic takes place, which sounds kind of crazy, but you have been preparing yourself for this by asking the four previous questions. You are ready. It is like putting all the freshly harvested ingredients together for a delicious meal and you turn on the heat. We have set the stage and cleared the way to be able to imagine that different is possible—something possibly bigger and better.

Hope lives here, courage can be invited and rallied from here, and grace thrives here. When we can create and envision what we hope for, all kinds of forces work behind the scenes to assist us in moving toward that. You send out an invitation to the universe declaring yourself ready and inviting it into the realm of possibilities to engage with you. This is the playground for what is possible in your life and that takes faith, which for me is sometimes challenging.

Morning Glories

I had spent time in my garden one morning planting the seeds of my favorite flower, morning glories. As I opened the seed packet, I was struck by the description on the back which read:

This vigorous and showy vine produces masses of sky blue flowers, many with contrasting white throats. (It can grow to 40 feet high.) Deep green foliage (with heart shape leaves) is perfect for beautiful fencing, arbors and trellises.

PLANTING: Select a sunny location with average soil. Plant after all danger of frost has past. Keep soil moist while plants are young.

NOTE: Morning glories bloom best in poor soil with a moderate water and no fertilizer.

This spoke to me so boldly that I saved that seed package and still have it 15 years later.

That is one of the most resilient, determined, vibrant plants on earth, I thought.

That was when I realized that I have the soul of a morning glory. If I were a flower, I would surely be a morning glory.

When I was in training to become a professional coach in 2000, we were asked to develop a Life Purpose statement. This is the statement that I developed that day to describe my purpose in life:

Plant me in average soil, though poor soil will do. I do need plenty of sun to feed my soul.

Give me enough water to survive and don't worry about fertilizing me, I will handle that. Then get out of my way.

I will reach toward the sun with my gorgeous blooms that open each morning to shout out their beauty and wonder to the world, sharing hope and vitality amidst their large, abundant heart-shaped leaves.

I will direct my energies every day to bloom, grow, and share glory and grace to the world wherever I am planted.

Fifteen years later, I still plant morning glories every year. They bring a smile to my face each summer morning as I walk out the door and they remind me of the expansive possibilities available in all of us—all from one tiny seed.

I plant them in places other than my garden—places I don't even own. They are a glorious, unexpected surprise for others and I want to see them growing there when I walk by. They are an unstoppable inspiration quietly elevating the spirit of others.

A Life Purpose statement moves you beyond what you think is realistic to what you feel is possible. It breaks through your limiting beliefs to empowering beliefs and ties your values, talents, strengths, passion, and purpose together in an image that embodies all that. Questions that help you to uncover your Life Purpose statement may include:

What am I really good at and enjoy doing?

What do others seek me out for?

What makes me feel alive?

What are my passions?

What matters most to me?

What really bothers me? (That can help just as much!)

A good coach can help you to create a statement that articulates meaning and purpose for you.

I hold onto the magic of morning glories by planting, photographing, and painting pictures of them. Their beauty and power remind me of my own inner beauty, power, and resilience and I am determined to bloom wherever my seeds are scattered and take root. This vision sustains me through rough times.

In this step of Grace Trail, you can use your imaginations, put aside your fears, and embrace all that is possible for you. I picture this as a bridge from where you are right now to where you want to go.

Are You a Good Witch or a Bad Witch?

One fall evening as I was starting to make dinner, I realized I needed something else at the store. As I drove up the street, I looked up at the beautiful full moon hanging over a field of tall grass next to the road, making moon shadows everywhere. In my car's headlights, I noticed something weird floating across the street. I squinted trying to figure it out as my headlights glinted off these strange objects.

What the heck is that? I thought, trying to determine what was right in front of me. The vision was so different from anything I had ever seen that my brain had nothing to compare it to. Puzzled, I drove closer and could see shiny, transparent blobs moving slowly ahead of me.

I stopped my car and directly in front of it were huge, 6-foot bubbles wafting across the road. These bubbles were like nothing I have ever seen, moving like giant jelly fish through the air.

"Giant bubbles," I muttered, "What is going on?"

As I looked to my left there in the middle of the field was a figure standing and waving something in her hand. I had to stop, roll down my window, and shout, "What are you doing?"

Of course, she replied, "Blowing bubbles."

Short pause.

"Can I join you?" I shouted.

"Sure!" she answered.

I parked the car and trudged through the field to where she was blowing her bubbles. Imagine: full moon, a field of long grass, and a mysterious stranger blowing giant bubbles. This is so magical, definitely not your average moment.

"Why are you doing this?" I foolishly asked the bubble witch all the while thinking, *Why wouldn't she be doing this?* and then, *Why isn't everyone here doing this?*

She went on to explain that she was practicing for the *Guinness Book of World Records'* largest bubble contest taking place in two days. She was a single parent with a young child and had gotten a babysitter for an hour so she could come to the field because she knew the conditions were perfect for blowing bubbles.

"How did you start all this?" I asked. She explained that the previous year she wanted to have a great birthday party for her son but her budget was really limited. She thought of doing something with bubbles because that was about all she could afford, so she did some research and learned how to make big bubbles. It was such a success that other parents asked her to come to their kids' parties and blow monster bubbles.

The result of that party is that she now has a bubble business, has developed a product to sell at events, and is booked through the spring and summer.

Of course, I photographed this moment because was I afraid no one would believe it—not another fish story!

Curiosity, enthusiasm, playfulness, hard work, adventure, humor, and creativity are alive and well in that story. Hope is also alive in there. She could dream a better party for her son and though there would be obstacles, she moved forward with the confidence that she would figure it out as she went along. She started small and let the momentum build.

This is really not about the bubbles. It is about the energy this woman brings to her work that ignites the energy of those she meets. At that moment in the field, she was residing in the realm of possibility. A bubble is a great metaphor for this: a floating, fleeting, breath of fresh air that silently moves by. You can enjoy it if you stop to notice its changing shape, swirling surface colors and ethereal presence. Or you can totally miss it as you drive right through it.

When I give workshops, I often blow bubbles, and not just any bubbles. These bubbles are specially formulated so they don't break easily or quickly. I ask people to notice what is different about these bubbles. They hold all the beauty and essence of a bubble as they float, reflect the light, and are transparent—the only exception is breakability. These bubbles are resilient. That's what I hope for you when you walk the Grace Trail. Resiliency is essential for living through the ups and downs that come from living a full life that invites in all that is possible. That's what I want for you—be one tough bubble.

The Language of Embrace

Expansive . . . Energy . . . Enlighten . . . Enliven . . . Envision . . . Embrace

We can really fool ourselves with the stories we tell ourselves.

The Parrot

Over many years visiting my family in Florida, I observed a man at the beach with a parrot on his shoulder. He was often surrounded by people, chatting and taking pictures of him and the bird, but I never approached him. I figured I'd have to pay for a picture or some other gimmick. Well, I was wrong.

This day, I observed the parrot sitting in a tree and the man on a bench nearby. When someone approached, with questions, he walked over to the bird, put his hand up, and the parrot stepped onto his hand and onto his shoulder. He then walked to the bench and sat, chatting with the crowd.

My sister in-law told me, "He raised that parrot from an egg 15 years ago!"

"No!" I said, astonished and more curious now.

At this point the man was sitting on a bench and the parrot leaned over, putting his head next to the man's head very much in an affectionate way—like he was snuggling. People standing nearby said, "Awww." It was touching and telling about their unusual relationship.

I asked him about raising the parrot from an egg and he confirmed that was true. I asked him if he clipped his wings so he wouldn't fly away and he said no, he never clipped his wings. He has his full feathers and the ability to fly. He said the parrot never tries to fly away because, from the parrot's point of view, *his flock walks.*

What an amazing thought. *Does your flock walk?*

What the "flock" are you doing? Are you sitting on a branch somewhere when you could be flying?

The first thing that you must do to encourage this mindset of embracing possibilities is to notice from where you are speaking. Are you speaking from the downward spiral of negativity and self-imposed restriction that would sound like:

> "I can never do that."
>
> "That won't ever happen."
>
> "Who me? I am not smart enough to do that."
>
> "It is too late for me to do that."
>
> "Who am I to think I can fly?"

My husband and I laugh because he used to say, "It always rains on my day off." Or, "We can't go there, we will never find a parking space." Funny, in all my years on earth, I have never returned home due to a lack of a parking. We can spin some really powerful stories that will either keep us tethered to our limitations or untie us and set our dreams free.

I find that people tend to speak from the position of a hammer and a nail instead of the sweeping flow of a paintbrush when referring to their limiting conditions, when, indeed, sparks of possibility go unnoticed and are regularly stomped upon.

One of the favorite photographic images in my workshop presentation is of a young girl in Germany who, when her parents denied her request for a horse, just threw a saddle on her cow and rode it.

Fill the Seats

While volunteering at a large conference for a professional organization, I had the responsibility to oversee a program we were running that day. We had 300 potential seats available to conference attendees to receive some complimentary coaching at the end of the conference day. It was necessary for us to be at the registration window in the morning to invite, educate, and enroll conference participants to take advantage of this opportunity. One year, we did not have the coaches present to actively meet and encourage people in the morning and when I checked with the woman on logistics, she reported that we were 150 seats empty—basically, half full.

As her job is to make sure the operations of the day runs smoothly, her initial response was, "Let's inform 10 people that they will not be coaching today because we don't have the clients scheduled for them. We do not want to have any empty seats or waste any coaches' time." That made great logistical sense and she was doing her job just as she was being asked to do.

My response to her was, "No, we have to fill those seats. Empty seats are not an option."

Surprised, she said, "Okay. Fill the seats... how?"

We moved the operations emphasis to "all hands on deck" for enrollment with coaches standing, promoting, and engaging conference attendees about the benefits of coaching and sitting for a coaching session.

Needless to say, we filled those 300 seats.

Where are you speaking from? Is it

> "There is not enough for me."
> or
> "There is enough to go around for all of us."

You not only have to notice where you are speaking from but you then have to make a choice. This awareness will help you to decide what steps you can take to manage your limiting and possibly negative mindset. What in this reality can be changed? There certainly are circumstances that cannot be changed and the situation above was not negative. The managing coach was doing her job with a different perspective than mine. We had competing visions of what was possible and what was necessary. Our challenge is to determine when those circumstances are true and when they are merely our perspective. It may take a leap of faith and courage to begin to infuse not only your language but also your actions as you embrace a sense of hope and possibility.

The Light House

One spring morning, I woke up very early, and because I could not go back to sleep, I got up. Wide awake, I asked myself, "What can I do right now that I can't do later?" and that was when I decided to go and see the sunrise.

I left a note for my husband, got in my car, and drove 20 minutes to my favorite spot at a lighthouse on the ocean. I parked my car right at the sea wall and climbed to the top of the wall. I was a little nervous to be there alone in the dark and, though I didn't feel any danger, I stayed near my car for an easy getaway if necessary.

As I was standing there getting used to the dark, I noticed that I was not alone. To my right, I saw a lone figure who must have had the same idea to catch a sunrise. I squinted in the dark to make out the person who had a tripod set up and a large camera focused on the impending sunrise. I assessed the situation and decided danger was minimal to none because I figured, *How many serial killers get up at sunrise with a big expensive camera and a tripod?* I also knew I could make it to my car before he could ever reach me so I stayed right there on the sea wall.

I temporarily forgot about my neighbor as I was overcome by the most beautiful horizon I could ever imagine. Standing there in the cool breeze with the glowing ball of energy rising above the ocean and the sounds of waves breaking on the beach, I was totally immersed in this moment—awesome, expansive, inspiring, and riveting. These sunrise moments pass quickly and I was surprised at how fast the sun rose above the horizon line once it poked its head up.

When I decided it was time to leave, I looked at the sea wall and it seemed much higher and more challenging going down than when I initially climbed up. Rather than take my chance on the rather steep wall, I took the safer, flatter route directly past the other person, who was now moving his camera and equipment for a new shot and angle. As he was on the path back to my car, I once again assessed my choices and chance of meeting danger and then walked toward the stranger. We acknowledged each other and instead of hurrying in opposite directions, we began to chat.

That early morning has fed my vitality in so many ways and the ripples from that chance meeting go on even today. Not only did I get to experience nature in all its glory but I met a talented, generous photographer who shared his photos with me so I can share them with others.

As I rode home, I looked at all the houses still dark with everyone still in bed. I felt sorry for all those people still asleep who had missed this sunrise, all the inspiration and beauty beyond compare. Then I realized that this happens every day, in every neighborhood, on every street in the world, an equal opportunity for beauty, discovery, curiosity, and awe. The one requirement is that you get out of bed, show up anywhere with a view of the horizon, and open your eyes to this possibility. Grace offers an equal opportunity of beauty and inspiration for all.

Amazing grace.

I try to scare myself once a day by doing something that feeds my vitality and brings me one step closer to my preferred future vision and dream. Images like these feed my energy and give me the power to persevere and not give up when times get tough.

I find that I need to push myself to increase my discomfort tolerance, to try new things, to get comfortable being uncomfortable on my journey of discovery. Be aware that squirming is part of the deal. Inertia and fear can hold me in my chair, keeping me from following my curiosity and finding potential adventures that are waiting just for me. It is those adventures that are like fertilizer and give me the nutrients to bloom in my own life.

This wonderful realm of possibility is not a state of mind that you can live in all the time. It is the sweet spot of possibility—just like sunrise when the sun shines briefly above the horizon illuminating the world with golden light and life. Wonder has a short shelf life so don't miss a moment of precious curiosity and enthusiasm when they show up. They are fleeting gifts, like a floating bubble, that require you to notice them and creatively engage. You won't notice when this moment arrives with just your eyes; it will speak to you if you listen. Be on the lookout for it with your heart and soul. Wait until you feel a tickle from the universe and open yourself to what is available in that moment.

Find those sweet spots on the earth that make your heart sing and visit them as often as you can or need to. Let the universe fill you. Inspiration is a nutrient that has no limits to feeding your spirit.

If you can't get to a spot on earth that speaks to you then create one. I have a place behind a big planter of petunias and pansies on my front steps where I can sit, unseen by my neighbors and revel in the optimism and hope inspired by the early morning quiet. The sun warms me, the birds sing to me, and the breeze blows softly by. I sometimes sit out there during a summer rainstorm just enjoying the sound of the rain as it falls and feeds the earth. You can invite and encourage these moments as you find or create these spots in your world, too.

Become a seeker and collector of awe. You know when those moments arrive because you hear yourself and others saying, "Awhhh…" Don't wait until the knock on the door. I have never had an adventure come calling for me. I find I usually have to stand up, put on my shoes, open the door, and walk out.

My biggest act of self-love is to continue to pursue that which inspires me, feeds my curiosity, and enhances my love of adventure. From there so much is possible—and so, my friend, what can you embrace as possible?

This is like painting a picture with your words. Here's the paint brush. You choose the colors.

Switchbacks

Choose one of these and do it whenever you have the feeling that you aren't where you are supposed to be but you don't know where that is—or just not up to where you want to be in your life, wondering what else might be ahead for you. Try one of these microbursts to jog that brain of yours out of its old ruts and start to carve out new ways of being and start to move in the direction of a fuller life.

- At night go up to your bedroom a little earlier. Turn down the lights. Do some gentle body stretches for relaxation. Pray a little, chat a little, ramble a little, dream a little—whatever you do to connect yourself to your higher vision and higher power. No one is listening except the universe so you really can't go wrong. Now ask your brain to search while you are asleep for pathways to that future or that better place that you desire in your life. Ask your heart to help you to dream about that when you are asleep. Welcome in the love of the universe to inform you of what you need to find your way there. Have a pencil and paper available so you can save whatever you hear, feel, or dream possible.

- On some mornings, do not get out of bed immediately when you awaken. Turn the alarm on earlier so you can delay jumping into action and turning your brain to "go" mode. Lay in bed and relish the time and space between sleep and being fully awake. This precious time in between your states of consciousness can be a time for the universe and your intuition to have an opportunity to finally be heard by you without the competing noise of your brain and your life. It is like planning daydreaming and then capturing all it has to offer you. Enjoy the energy of unedited, free flowing, creative thoughts.

- Doodle. Then doodle some more. Grace Trail doodling. Doodle the questions, doodle the answers, and doodle the trail that you desire. Experience the energy of floundering forward, safely on paper, not knowing with any certainty where you are headed.

- Become a seeker of awe. Find those sweet spots on earth that speak to you and open your heart to places and things that fill you with that feeling of awe. This may be an art show, a concert, a special place, anything that elevates your heart. Go there often for a tune-up. Let go and do some "awake dreaming" while you are there.

- As a child, what did you do that you enjoyed? When did you lose track of time? Laugh? Connect? Create? Play? Do that again as often as possible. Experience the energy of flow.

- Go to a playground and swing on the swings. Immerse yourself in the sensory experience and do not think. Enjoy the energy of freedom.

- Skip. Don't walk. Swing your arms and smile. Better to do this in the dark when you won't feel so self-conscious or in a quiet place where you won't be observed. For those of you who don't care about others opinions or judgments, skip anywhere and anytime you feel like skipping. Feel the energy of outrageousness awaken inside of you.

- Go for a "trust walk" with someone you really trust. Find a place where you can walk and not be observed closely or overheard by others. Ask this person to safely navigate for the both of you as you hold onto their arm and they lead you as you close your eyes and walk. Experience going forward into the unknown, knowing you will be okay walking, wandering, and wondering. (I close my eyes on some straight stretches of the trail and let my dog Willie guide me.)

- Say "bonjour" to everyone that you pass on a busy street. Say it with a twinkle in your eye and the voice of someone who is playful, thoroughly enjoying themselves and wickedly adventurous. Anything is possible in Paris. Connect with others around the energy of fun and enthusiasm.

- Walk outside and listen to the birds. Imagine what they would see if they were to look down on your life? What do they see as possible for you? What type of bird represents the essence of you? Allow some new perspectives to enter.

- One cloudless night, look for shooting stars. Remind

yourself that you live on a planet. Experience the energy of awe.

- Notice what makes you feel alive and gives you hope so you can make it happen more often. Keep noticing and feeling for that and watch what makes it more intense and pleasurable.

- Get yourself to a sunrise. This is an equal opportunity of possibility for all to breathe in the wonder and glory of the moment. You just have to wake up, stand up, and show up to claim your space. Declare it yours. Stand tall in it.

- Embrace that you are worthy of choosing your next step toward your destiny. You have taken the 5 steps toward your best life and this is your invitation to you to **embrace** all that is possible.

Here is a visualization that may help you:

Stand with your feet apart and take three deep breaths.

Put your head back, imagine the sun on your face, and slowly, in your mind, move down your body and loosen the tightness you find there.

Put your arms out to your side and gently shake them out, relax them, and picture shaking your anxieties off.

Breathe.

In your mind, go to a place that makes you feel empowered, secure, and connected to the best the world has to offer—a mountaintop, a beach, a spot in your garden.

Throw your arms out wide and put your head back as you breathe in and ask yourself . . .

What can I embrace as possible from here? Give yourself time and then listen.

What do you see?

What do you hear?

What do you feel?

Questions to take with you on the Trail

1. Where do I wish to focus my energies right now?

   What is the impact that I desire?

2. What captures my attention in life and gives me hope? What image repeatedly speaks to me about me overcoming obstacles? And now, how can I use this as a guide for where I want to point my life energies?

3. Who would I be if I let the world know who I am instead of who I think I should be?

4. What makes me feel alive?

    How can I get more of that?

5. Sometimes I push things away or brace against them.

    What do I want to both invite in and allow in, instead of resisting?

    What if I stop pushing it away, open my arms, and let life happen?

    What is possible?

Final Thoughts

As you have noticed by now, ocean stones or any water weathered stones have meaning to me and a message for us all. Each one is a work of art that makes them unique and ever changing. They are millions of years old and not only witnesses to earth's mighty and tumultuous evolution but active partners in these changes. That is what I want for you on Grace Trail: to be an active, resilient, vibrant partner in the life you wish to create and were meant to live.

At The Water's Edge©

Just like you,
these stones have been through some mighty storms,
rolled and tossed at the water's edge.
But they endure and make it through
with softer edges
and smoother surfaces,
their colors clear and true.
Still here on the beach,
rolling with the next wave.

by Anne Jolles

This is it. This is the life you have right now. We can't change what has happened in our life but we can choose how we go forward from here.

It is so easy to be busy but so challenging to be consciously living your life in the direction of your choice. All of us are capable of living so much more of our life awake and alive by engaging more moments with curiosity and conscious choices.

As crazy as the world and your day seems, getting yourself together and back in touch with you and your feelings, helps the world. The more you stop the distractions and craziness inside of you and around you by listening to your inner wisdom and answers, the more connected and grounded you will be with yourself and others. Then things start to change and that is where hope lies.

You can live your life and invite grace into your life more often. Grace Trail can help you to find meaning and opportunity in the chaos of your life.

Grace is all around us. We can notice it, invite it, create circumstances that attract it, and, gratefully, sometimes it just shows up.

Bring these Grace Trail questions inside to where the answers are just waiting for you to find them.
Grace is not always graceful but it is always worth it.

Here's my wish for you:

At those times when you think you have forgotten all that you once knew, feel distracted and lost, or, even worse, think you know everything . . .

Start to walk Grace Trail.

Look around your life and cherish all that is positive, true, and strong. Elevate your perspective with **gratitude** as you plant your feet firmly on what is going right in your life.

Loosen your grip on fear, scarcity, and all that is out of your control and open your heart in just this moment. Picture yourself putting the heavy load down and **releasing** that burden at least for a while and possibly forever.

As your vision becomes clearer, be gentle on yourself and quietly observe all that is around you and inside of you—considering that you are exactly where you are meant to be. Know that **acceptance** does not mean you have to like the situation or that you have given up. It encourages choices.

Rest there, breathe, and ask, *What's my **challenge?** Where do I wish to focus my precious energies?*

Listen to your answer and choose your next step.

Then stand, throw your arms out wide, put your head back, and open your heart to **embrace** all that is hopeful and possible in this moment. Focus your attention and intentions toward that point on the horizon that entices you forward toward the life you were meant to live.

And live forward from there.

From my heart to yours,

This trail is for you...

Anne Jolles

Acknowledgments

This book would not exist without the contributions of the following people. They each shared bits and pieces of an amazing puzzle that has somehow come together as the book I always wanted to write about The Grace Trail.

Each of the following people loved it or loved me in a way that encouraged me to move forward. Or discouraged me enough to figure it out. And for that I am so grateful.

Thank you to...

Jon, Rob, and Lex for walking this winding trail as a family.

My parents for loving us with all they had, and my siblings.

Ginny Maness and Dawn Williams for being my "encouragers supreme". They always discovered the nuggets of truth and wisdom no matter how small and brought their fresh, honest perspectives.

Tracy Mindess for her support and editing of my early writing.

Jackie Jolles Siegel for being comforted by holding those stones...

Susan Radin for all those miles we walked together.

Loretta LaRoche, Michelle Spinale, Maryann Cavicchi, Therese Heney, Karen Burke, Stephanie Marisca, Karen Senteio, Paul Kandarian, Chelsea Franklin, Millie Grenough, Laurie McAnaugh for their invaluable support and contributions. And Janet Finnegan Kelly and Pat Pharr for bringing the trail west.

All of my neighbors and trail walkers in Plymouth.

Steve Harrison and Bill Harrison, Geoffrey Berwind, Martha Bullen, and all of the Quantum Leap coaches and staff.

Tracy Grigoriades for guiding me through the details and holding the big picture for me.

Lindsey Alexander and Heidi Grauel for their editing, Laura Duffy for her cover design, Deana Riddle for her interior book design and Jill Powell for her map and drawings.

The many walkers and stewards of Grace Trail... wherever that trail may be.

About the Author

Anne Barry Jolles is Boston born and raised. She graduated from Boston University with a degree in Occupational Therapy and went on to receive an MBA from the Simmons Graduate School of Management. Following her heart, Anne was led to the Coaches Training Institute to receive her coaching education and certification. She has been a professional life coach for 15 years and was proud to be selected as International Coach Federation of New England Life Coach of the Year in 2013. Anne coaches people all over the world to help make their creative passions and aspirations a reality.

Anne has been married to her husband and best friend, Jon, for almost 40 years. Together, they raised their children, Rob and Alexa.

Anne loves to walk, bike, kayak, dance, paint, and float in an inner tube whenever possible. She keeps an eye out for a good adventure and tries to bring curiosity, compassion, and a light heart to most situations.

Anne's mission is to spread inspiration, optimism, and resiliency to the world with the intention of elevating as many hearts as possible. Through her coaching work and creation of Grace Trail, she seems to be doing just that.

A portion of the proceeds from this book goes to the Wounded Warrior Project, an organization dear to Anne's heart and part of the inspiration for the Grace Trail.

Connect with Anne Barry Jolles and the Grace Trail

A Gift for You:

Please enjoy Anne's inspirational short story, "Walking Off Your War," as a thank you. This story is about a survivor who makes it through her personal war by walking her own Grace Trail back to hope and possibility. To receive your free PDF download, you can access your copy at her website, www.gracetrail.com.

Bring Anne Jolles and the Grace Trail to You:

Anne Barry Jolles is available for speaking, coaching, seminars, workshops, retreats and other engagements. Anne can also design a Grace Trail for your organization or conference. If you are interested in learning more about her inspiring programs — or would like to set up a consultation about how you can bring the Grace Trail to your town or organization — contact Anne at abjcoach@icloud.com. Bulk discounts of the book are also available.

Did You Like Grace Trail?

Thank you so much for your purchase of this book. If you enjoyed it, please consider writing a brief review on Amazon, so that other readers can benefit from the Grace Trail. Many thanks!